SOME MEMORIES OF CALIFORNIA
(A MEMOIR)

DIPO KALEJAIYE

SOME MEMORIES OF CALIFORNIA. Copyright © Dipo Kalejaiye, 2017.

CISSUS WORLD PRESS
ISBN: 978-0-9978689-5-1
Distributor: African Books Collective
www.africanbookscollective.com

Chapter 1: Prologue or the 'Escape'.

The metaphysical event which led to my leaving Nigeria and coming back to the United States is worth enumerating. Prior to this particular event, it is necessary to look at the chronology of events which even led to the metaphysical one. As the saying goes in the Yoruba language, "*A ti ibi pelebe la tin mu ole je*". That is, "it is from the very edges of a bean cake (moin moin), that one starts to eat it." I want to start from the "edges of the bean cake" in order to show what prompted me to leave Nigeria for the United States.

The situation which caused what I can regard as my 'escape' was the eeriest one in which I had ever found myself. Why did I abandon a fairly comfortable university teaching position in Nigeria, for the United States, when I had not made any plans for such a sudden comeback? For example, I had not secured a teaching position in the United States prior to my leaving Nigeria and I did not even make any arrangement for accommodation since I had been out of the country for about five years. But when the incident that prompted my departure from the university and Nigeria occurred, I was sure that I had no choice but to leave abruptly as I did. The abruptness was so complete it was even a wonder to me. I sold my Volkswagen Passat at a very cheap price and used the money to buy a one-way plane ticket to the United States. As it was then, I had a fairly middle-class kind of position complete with the honour and prestige that went with it. One voice inside me told me that perhaps what I was about to do was really not the answer to the problem which drove me out of the university and the country, but another voice inside me was louder and emphatic. It said: "Go… do not listen to anyone. Follow your instincts and get out of the country now". I was quite comfortable. I had a car, a teaching position in the Department of Theatre Arts as a Lecturer 11, a government subsidized accommodation on campus, which was a four bedroom flat complete with a Boys' Quarters, and a loving family. The event I am about to narrate is not spurious in any way. The incident happened this way.

I had just returned from a small vacation in Lagos in 1984. It was a long drive of about six to seven hours from Lagos back to Calabar. That evening I wanted to get to my office to begin work on two short comedies, *Polygamy* and *Polyandry* (later published as *Polygyny and Polyandry: Two Plays about Marriage* by Macmillan Publishers, London, in 1985). My wife begged me not to go to the office that day as we had just returned from a strenuous road trip and that I needed to rest. I ignored her warning. I was always in the habit of following my instincts when it came to writing. If I got an urge to write when someone was talking to me, I would break off from the conversation politely, and go to an isolated place to write. Jumoke knew about my writing habit. At the time, it was usual for me to be alone when I wrote. Since it was a Sunday, the office would provide the solace in writing because no one would be there. Even Dexter Lyndersay, a man of about seven feet tall, the then Head of Department, and a workaholic was away in his country of Trinidad on vacation. I entered my office, the one I shared with Dr. Peter Nwankwo, an Igbo man whose intense tribalism was a shock to me. I could not fathom how someone who had gotten his Ph.D. in education from a university in South Carolina in the United States could be so narrow-minded. I could not reconcile "tribalism" with "academics." He was a rather cunning individual who reminded me so much of the cunning tortoise in Yoruba folktales. In fact, his conversations with me which were often fake and tenuous usually made my skin crawl. He would tease me that I was so talented and young and that I would soon be the "youngest professor from *Ilupeju*" in the Department of Theatre Arts. Those words reverberated in my mind. What does that mean? "The youngest professor from *Ilupeju*".

Yes, I was young, about thirty, when I became a Lecturer 1 at the University of Calabar in Nigeria. At the time, being a professor was not in my mind as much as my writing.

He and three others were a gang of four who were tribalistic in their way of doing things. They were always talking about how "talented" I was and they marveled that at twenty-five, I had won first prizes in American literary awards such as The Ina Coolbirth Prize for Poetry and The James D. Phelan Literary Award for Playwriting. Of course, the seamy jealousy reached a troubling proportion when I plastered the cover of one of my published plays which won the Phelan Award, *The Father of Secrets*, on my notice board behind my desk in the office. Also, when Centaur Press Calabar published my play, *The Creator and the Disrupter,* I placed the cover of the published play on my notice board as well. A few months later, Chris Dunton, a respected scholar in African Literature with an interest in Nigerian drama, wrote a favourable review of the play which appeared in the then influential magazine – *West Africa*. Again, I placed the clipping of this review on my notice board. To make matters worse, Dr. Nwankwo and his gang were incensed when on August 16, 1982, I was chosen by the department of Theatre Arts to direct a departmental production of the classical Greek comedy – *Lysistrata*. They had fought vigorously at a departmental meeting to prevent my being chosen as the one to direct the play. The then head of the department, Francis E. Speed, who took over temporarily after Lyndersay was 'hounded' out, by the tribalists, wrote an official letter to me dated 16th August 1982, He wrote:

Further to our discussion in the Production Committee and agreement in the departmental meeting of Friday 13th August, I am asking you to produce Lysistrata for showing in the new theater 2nd to 6th December 1982. I am confident that the production will be a success in the hands of an experienced director such as you have proved to be. (Official letter from Francis E. Speed ref # UC/TA/ 421 of 16th August 1982)

I modified the play somewhat, using Nigerian Pidgin English as the language spoken by Kaloninke and Myrrhine, the husband and wife in the play. Here is an excerpt from a review of the production by Rom J. Celsius, which appeared in a newspaper.

One thing that strikes one immediately the play opens is the use of Pidgin English by Lampito, (played by Obioma Ijeoma Offonry); however, the Director explained that he used the Duddley Fitts' translation of Lysistrata. In this translation, Fitts used Black American English to replace a Greek dialect used in the original Greek version. It gave a lot of verbal colour to the play and demonstrates directorial ingenuity. Lysistrata's carriage on stage is impressive and reflects her as the tough born to lead woman she is in the play. By the use of the phallic symbol, the Director, Mr. Dipo Kalejaiye has shown a deep knowledge of Greek theater. The set was very Greek in nature, and impressive. The placement of the Chorus on the stage instead of the orchestra pit as in the conventional Greek theater enhanced the beauty of the play. The music was very good. (The Sunday Call February 6, 1983.)

The production was a huge success. I modified the play somewhat, using Nigerian Pidgin English as the language spoken by Kaloninke and Myrrhine, the husband and wife in the play. I followed it with the production of my original play, *Messamba,* which I was simultaneously writing even as I was battling the grueling rehearsals for *Lysistrata.* (Unfortunately, because of my numerous relocations, I have lost the manuscript of *Messamba*!). The play was really an absurdist socio-political satire of metaphysical proportions with characters such as Honourable Minister, Managing Director, Philosopher, Patriot, Chairman, Female Activist, Oracle Priest, Beggars, and Hungry Citizens. Ime Ikiddeh a lecturer in the Department of English at the time came to see the production of the play, and he sent me a written criticism of it this way:

I do not think anyone would miss the close relevance of the subject of this play to our contemporary social and political situation. The representation is real, sometimes too painfully real in spite of much of the surface humour. I found the dialogue or at least a good deal of it credible in its attempt to capture the particular social reality that is the concern of the author. I thought the set was well chosen, simple and unobtrusively effective. I was particularly impressed by the promptness of entries, the briskness of scene changes, not altogether strong features of our past productions at UNICAL. (A criticism of the play from Ime Ikiddeh, Lecturer in English and Literary Studies Department, titled "Messamba: A commentary". University of Calabar 1981)

On the other hand, I received a personal letter from Sister Eileen Sweeney, an Irish Nun who was also a lecturer at the University of Calabar's English and Literary Studies Department at the time, and who also saw the production she wrote:

This is an interesting play written as a satire of a perennial political and social situation where the administration has become an alienating institution, instead of an enabling one, and whose repressive and oppressive actions and omissions have created and continue to sustain an unstable and unjust situation. I found that the Philosopher carried the burden of explicating the theme. He was well satirized as a man unable to make up his mind or rise to a challenge. I did not find that it was a lack of dramatic skill that left the ending inconclusive rather; I found it deliberately thought provoking. (Personal letter from Sister Eileen Sweeney, Department of English, University of Calabar, July 20, 1981.)

The then Dean of Arts, Professor Ernest Emenyonu, congratulated me on the success of *Lysistrata* during one of our Faculty of Arts meetings. About this time, 1982 to 1983, the department was simmering with petty tribalism. The tribalists felt that a Nigerian should head the Department of Theater Arts in a Nigerian university. They thought that Lyndersay, a Trinidadian, and Speed, a British citizen, were not qualified to "head" the department. If one was from the 'wrong' tribe, that is, if one was not Efik or Ibibio, two of the tribes in the Cross River State, then, one was automatically opposed by the gang of four and their sympathizers. Of course, there was another school of thought which believed that an "Igbo man" should head the department. Miraculously, Kalu Uka, an Igbo man, surfaced from the University of Nsukka and he took over from Frank Speed – the British. Who were these "gang of four?" They were the Mafia who cunningly wielded tribal power over the department. The members of the gang were Dr. Peter Nwankwo, Mr. Sonny Johnson Enok, Mr. Pino Abang, and Mr. Alex Koropam.

The youngest professor from *Ilupeju*? I was not from "*Ilupeju*" at all. Ilupeju was an area in Lagos. I was really from *Ogere*, a small town forty-five miles to Lagos. For Peter, to be a Yoruba was synonymous with being from *Ilupeju*. This was an obvious stereotypical notion. Well, he was not in the office the day I went there to write. I was elated; I could have the office to myself. I sat down at my desk and began to write. It was not long before my body started to itch so badly. I didn't know why. It was unusual. I packed up and left the office in a hurry. I did not know if my butter colour Volkswagen Passat drove itself or I drove it to my abode at the university staff quarters. I ran inside and peeled off my clothes screaming and scratching like a disoriented child. Jumoke, my wife, maintained her calm. To me, she was always calm in any situation. I was usually exasperated by that because I thought she was always 'too calm' for comfort. The white part of my eyeball had turned totally red. I was rolling on the floor of the living room crying like a baby! I told Jumoke not to let me die! I told her that I had been a victim of juju! In her characteristic manner of remaining 'unusually calm and logical' in the face of any problem or emergency, she chastised me for "acting like a child" and that I was probably allergic to the combination of beer and corn I had just before I drove to the office.

 My friend, Dr. Anthony Ike Nwajei, an Igbo man, and a wonderful individual, who was refined, charismatic, and intensely kind, was the resident medical doctor at the University of Calabar at the time. He told me that he could not help me because the symptom seemed "odd and unusual" and incompatible with everything he knew about western medicine. He said: "Look my friend; I think this is *juju,* I can't help you". He spoke in impeccable Yoruba. (He had been raised in Lagos and had attended secondary school there.) "You will have to go the native way to have the metaphysical spell removed" he concluded. I panicked. Here was a man trained in western medicine who also believed in the power of African juju (or evil spell). I thought that was brilliant. He was a perfect blend of the traditional and the modern and a pragmatist to the core. Later, that evening, as I was still reeling in the agony of the metaphysical spell, he came to my flat and told my wife that since western medicine couldn't cure me we would have to try Yoruba traditional medicine. We resolved that I must go back to Lagos quickly for a traditional cure.

I had chosen the wrong day to travel out of Calabar. The Nigerian Medical Association was having their annual convention in Calabar, and therefore there was a shortage of planes flying out of the airport to Lagos. It seemed to me that the doctors had commandeered all available planes! Essentially, one must be a medical doctor in order to fly out of Calabar to Lagos that day. I had to virtually force myself into one, agreeing to pay extra, and to sit on the floor in the aisle of the plane just so that I can reach Lagos that day! I didn't want to die. I looked at my two daughters, Bola, who was only three years old, Buki who was two years, and my son Yinka, who was about nine months old, and concluded that they were much too young to be fatherless.

I arrived in Lagos and I went straight to a member of my extended family, a woman who was quite knowledgeable about metaphysical spells. As I approached her building, I saw some busybody tenants of the adjoining building come out to stand on the balcony overlooking the street. They were looking at me, obviously enjoying my predicament, and pointing at me. I even heard some of them giggling and laughing! One of them had to grab his two-year-old son and placed him on his shoulder so that he too could see the spectacle I had become. I was ashamed. That was the same street I used to approach with pride and dignity whenever I came to see this particular relative. The thoughts going through the mind of the tenants seemed to me to be something like: "That serves you; right… you thought you were better than us… you university lecturers who are always speaking in English even when someone would talk to you in Yoruba". I snapped out of my surreal thought. Perhaps they were not thinking all of that after all. But they were all standing on that balcony looking at me and struggling with each other to get a better viewing spot. I was scratching my body and walking as if someone had tied a rope around my two legs and forced me to keep walking all the same.

When I reached my relative's house, I stumbled into the car garage and collapsed at the entrance to the downstairs flat where she lived. One of her two maids, a girl with tribal marks, and who was only sixteen at the time, took one look at me and ran back inside as if she had seen a ghost! My relative, Mrs. Konjo, appeared holding the door leading to her flat open for me. She was calm, smiling, and unperturbed! Then, she looked at me in the most curious way and said: "So you university lecturers also practice juju?" She said laughing in a sarcastic manner. I was angry. How did she know that I was suffering from a juju spell? Why was she laughing? I didn't think that the matter was a laughing matter at all. I believed that I was dangling between life and death, and no one should be laughing about that. She asked the question again, "I said so you university lecturers also practice juju? I thought juju was only associated with the illiterates and the lowly class?" I was not in a position to answer her as I was scratching my body so much I thought I would scratch to the bone. She looked at me and said nonchalantly "You are not going to die, don't worry". Her husband, a stark illiterate, but incredibly wealthy, initially seemed unsympathetic towards me. The man, Alhaji Konjo, owned about twenty houses in Lagos and was a contractor at the Lagos port involved in the clearing and forwarding of imported goods. He took one look at me and went to sit in his massive living room which looked like three sitting rooms rolled into one. What was wrong with Alhaji Konjo? Was he not concerned with my predicament? Why did he abandon me in the corridor to go and sit in his living room? He then ordered that he should be served, Guinness Stout. I saw the maid with tribal marks, Moji, bring him the Guinness Stout and peppered smoked meat. When I saw him drinking the stout and eating the peppered smoked meat, I was incensed. Surely this man did not care about a man about to die who was sitting in his corridor and scratching his body uncontrollably. Minutes elapsed and my indignance grew to a boiling point. Just when I had given up on Alhaji, I heard him call his wife, Alhaja, in his usual husky voice and instructed her to take me to see an Ifa priest who lived in the Ebutte Meta area of Lagos. My relative, Mrs. Konjo, was affectionately referred to as

"*Alhaja,*" because upon the instruction of her husband, she had made the holy pilgrimage to Mecca. She took her time getting dressed, eyeing me coyly. I thought that was a deliberate attempt to make sure I was dead before I got to the Ifa priest! Why was this woman playing with such a serious matter? I pleaded with her to please hurry up and get dressed, but she continued to take her time and even called Moji to bring her lunch, which she ate in the slowest manner I had ever seen anyone eat in my life. There seemed to be an incredibly long time between one morsel and the other, and she took forever to pick up her glass of water to drink it, and to place it down again. I pleaded with her again to hurry. When she finished eating, she took her time to put on her makeup, doing it in a slow manner as she had done when she was eating. Looking at me and seeing my exasperation, she said: "What is the matter with you? Are you going to be the first one to be afflicted with an evil juju spell? Why are you such a coward? Can't you just be a man for a minute?" I shuddered. "Be a man for a minute?" I thought. I did not intend to be brave in the face of that impending tragedy. So, I decided to leave her alone. At least I was in her house. If I died, I would have done so in a relative's house. Moments later, she got up, and walked into her bedroom, got dressed and took me to see a *Babalawo* (a priest of Ifa – the Yoruba god of divination). On the way to the Ifa priest, she kept up a barrage of questions concerning my condition. I did not answer any one of them. I was still upset with her for taking her time in getting me to the Ifa priest. I fixed my gaze on the snarling traffic on the ever- congested Lagos road. "Why did you not go to your mother in Ibadan?" She asked. I did not answer that question either as I was worried that if I did that, the issue of my joblessness and homelessness would come out and I would be regarded as a failure. Everyone would know the exact thing I was trying to hide. I really wanted to leave Nigeria without a lot of people knowing that I had left! I took care to warn those who knew about my impending weird disappearance such as my wife, and Alhaja Konjo, to keep the matter to themselves. Eventually, I got their cooperation in this regard.

The Ifa priest was the most sophisticated one I had ever met. He was about fifty years, stoutly built, and with tribal marks. He lived in the Ebutte Meta area of Lagos. His two room tenement was sparkling clean. He even had a working refrigerator, a radio, and a television set. He wore a gold watch, which sparkled endlessly, and he seemed to smile perpetually. He was constantly eating kola nuts and telling his wives to drive off the stray goats that were bleating in his backyard, as he did not want them to defecate there. He was a man obsessed with cleanliness. I thought he was classy; I was impressed.

It was afternoon. As soon as he saw us, he dismissed his two wives who were lurking around and asked my relative and me to sit down on a mat in front of him. He got up and turned on the ceiling fan as it was incredibly hot. Then, he folded the sleeves of his immaculate looking *agbada* outfit over his shoulders, brought out his divining chain often referred to as *opele* and began an eerie incantation. The incantation was entirely in the Yoruba language, but here is the English translation:

Was the one who casts Ifa for the monkey? (Oun l'o d'ifa fun Obo)
When he was going to visit his in-laws (Nigbati o nrele awon ana re)
They said he should sacrifice (A ni ki o rubo)
And he would not see evil (A ni ko ni r'ibi)
We asked him to sacrifice: (A ni ko rubo)
 Two bales of white cloth (Iro aso funfun meji)
A pigeon (Eieyele)
 Plenty of corn meal (Opolopo eko)
Several chickens (Opolop adie)
Two he-goats (Obuko meji)
Two eggs-laying ducks (Pepeiye meji)
Kola nuts (Obi)
Bitter kola (Orogbo)
Guinea fowl (Awo)
 And palm wine. (Emu)
They said he should wake up early (A ni ki o ji ni kutukutu owuro)
And worship his head (Ki o bo ori re)
They said that (A wipe)
If one's head cannot save one from danger (Bi Ori eni ko ba le gbe ni)
Nothing can (Ko si ohun ti o le gbe ni)

The monkey was busy playing with its tail   (Obo nfi iru re sere)
We told the monkey: "Worship the head not the tail
"(A wipe ki o bo Ori re ki ise iru re)
But that day, it was its tail   (Sugbon ni ojo na)
The monkey chased around   (Iru re ni ifi sere)
Like a foolish dog   (Bi aja omugo)
He kept playing with its tail.   (O nfi iru re sere)
On his way   (Nigbati nlo)
 To his in-laws   (S'ile awon ana re)
 Ah! Avoiding death twice!   (Ah! Oyeku Meji)

Oh mothers of the night   (Eyin iya mi Osolonga)
Owners of the amulet of silver   (Alado ide)
The finicky birds that fly at midday   (Afinju eiye ti nfo losan
gangan)
The finicky birds that fly at midnight   (Afinju eiye ti nfo l'oru
oganjo)
Look at me with approving eyes   (E f'oju re wo mi o)
For it is with approving eyes   (Nitori oju re)
That we look at money   (La fi now owo)
Look at me with approving eyes   (E f'oju re wo mi o)
The one who says what will you become?   (Eni t'o so pe ki l'e o
da?)
The one who says where is your power?   (Eni t'o so pe agbara
nyin da)
Is like the one   (O dabi eniti)
Who foolishly jumps into the river?   (O f'o s'odo)
But cannot swim   (Ti ko si mo we)
Who does not know?   (Ta ni ko mo wipe)
That his foolishness   (Omugo re)
Will make him   (Yio je ki)
Drown in the river?   (O ku sinu odo?)
Oh mothers of the night   (Enyin iya mi to ni
ale)
Owners of the amulet of silver   (Enyin alado ide)

I pay homage to you	(Mo juba nyin o!)
Look at me with approving eyes	(E f'oju re wo mi o)
I say it is with approving eyes	(Mo ni oju re)
That we look at money	(La fi now owo)
Look at me with approving eyes	(E f'oju re wo mi o)
Ah! Running away twice!	(Ah! Osa Meji)

We cast Ifa for the ostrich	(A difa fun Ogongo)
We told the ostrich to beware	(A wifun Ogongo wipe ki o sora)
And it would not see evil	(Ko si ni ri ibi)
We said: "Do not rely on your long neck"	(A ni ki o ma se gb'oju le orun re gigun)
For you cannot see everything	(Nitoripe ko le ri gbogbo nkan tan)
The ostrich was busy	(Ogongo nfi)
Playing with its beautiful feathers.	(Iye re daradara sere)
She was showing off	(On nfi iye re yangan)
For the world to see	(Fun gbogbo ara aye ri)
But the name of *Orunmila* is *Olugini*	\(Sugbon Oruko Orunmila ni Olugini)
His name is *Ejiogbe*	(Oruko re ni Ejiogbe)
That is the name of the father of Ifa	(Eyiyi ni Oruko Ifa)
When dawn breaks	(Nigbati ti ojumo ba mo)
I hear not the crowing of cocks	(Ngo gbo ki akuko ko)

Morning breaks	(Nigbati ti ojumo ba mo)
I see no dew drops	(Ngo ri eeri ki o se)
It will land, it will land,	(Yio b'ale yio b'ale)
Is all a child's wish	(Ni imo omode)
As the bird	(Titi eiye)
Enters the forest.	(Fi w'onu igbo)
It will land, it will land	(Yio b'ale yio b'ale)
Is only a futile wish.	(Ni imo asan)
Ah! He will meet him and buy	(Ah! Obara!)
The earthworm	(Nigbati ti ekolo)
Worships the ground	(Ba juba ile)
And the ground opens up	(Ile a l'anu)
It pays homage	(O juba)
And was king of the underground	(O si di Oba abe ile)
I say it pays homage	(O juba)
And the rain torrents	(Agbara ojo)
Does not sweep it away	(Ko wo lo)
It knows to pay homage	(O mo lati juba)
When a wife	(Nigbati ti Iyawo)
Pays homage to her husband	(Ba juba oko re)
The result is pregnancy	(Yio loyun!)
When we pay homage to *Orunmila*	(Nigbati a ba juba Orunmila)

If we pay homage to *Agbonniregun*	(Nigbati a ba juba Agbonniregun)
Our lives shall be long	(Emi wa yio gun)
On this earth	(L'ori ile aiye)
Orunmila	(Orunmila)
I pay homage today	(Mo juba loni o)
Orunmila the owner of Ile Ife	(Orunmila eniti o ni Ile Ife)
Where dawn breaks	(Nibi ojumo rere ti mo wa ile iye)
For the whole world to see	(Fun gbogbo aiye lati ri)
I pay my own homage today!	(Mo juba loni o!)
Let my life be long on earth	(Je ki aiye mi gun lori le aiyc yi)
Let me not see evil	(Mase je ki nri ibi)
And let evil not see me	(Ma si se je ki ibi ki o ri mi)
For evil is like a witch	(Ibi dabi awon iya mi Osolonga)
One who knows her will not see her	(Eniti o mo nwon ki yio ri nwon!)
And the one that sees her will not know her	(Eni ti o si ri nwon ki yio mo nwon!)
Orunmila I pay homage!	(Orunmila mo juba loni o!)
Let me not see evil today!	(Mase je ki nri ibi)
Let my life be long on earth	(Je ki npe lori ile aiye yi)
Ah! It is the second that I support	(Ah! Ejiogbe)

Baba Fatola, the Ifa Priest stopped. There was an eerie silence. Then, he looked at my relative, me, and then spoke in a measured tone.

"He will need two healthy he-goats, yes, they must be healthy, two egg-laying ducks, kola nuts, a guinea fowl, and bales of white cloth. We will use the blood of the he-goats to wash his head. Yes, where he works there are four people there. They are jealous of his accomplishments and have placed an evil *juju* on his chair in his office. The *juju* is supposed to make him go mad, but his head is so "strong" his fate repels evil, so the *juju* was unable to reach his brain. His head saved him. If the juju had reached his brain – no remedy, he would have gone incurably mad."

I had seen the numerous mad people in Calabar walking the streets naked and asking for money, and food. Usually, the mad people would say things like "*No mi ten kobo*" in Efik language (which meant "Give me ten kobo"). Essentially, I thought there were too many of them. It was at this time I found out that the famous method for settling a score with someone in Calabar was to purchase this very cheap *juju* get the person to come in contact with it and the person would go incurably mad. That was common knowledge in Calabar at the time, but I was totally naïve about this fact. "Four people," I thought um… the "gang of four, the tribalists". Immediately, I knew who they were. I was cured of the evil spell.

For some time, I was in hibernation in Lagos. I had no inkling as to how I could tell family members and friends, about the real incident which drove me out of the University of Calabar. I could not tell anyone that I had actually abandoned my teaching position and that I was jobless and homeless in Lagos! A former student of mine at the University of Calabar, Isaac Thorpe, found me or I found him, and he asked me why I left the university. I did not tell him the real reason I left. At the time, his sprawling family home was located somewhere on Herbert

Macaulay Way in Lagos and he asked me to come and stay there until my departure for the United States. He was generous to me, asking his mother to make sure that I ate at least two meals a day. He also arranged for me to live in the back of their main house, which was built like a Boys' Quarters with four rooms in it. My room was next to that of another young lady, Morenike, who was definitely a tenant of the Thorpe family. She was amazingly attractive, but was always dressed in a flamboyant manner with heavy makeup. She must have been aware of her beauty as she tried to tempt me with it. She would walk up to my door and try to start a conversation with me, but I was too pre-occupied with my predicament at the time to take any notice of her. Besides, I told her that I was married. She said she did not believe me and queried me that if I was married where was my wife? Since I was not about to open any Pandora's box by telling her about my affairs, I insisted I was married and that the relationship she was seeking would not work. That was when she tried to pick up fights with me which I cleverly avoided. She accused me of using the water which she had drawn from the public tap and placed in front of her room. I told her that I did not use her water but she did not accept the explanation. Finally, I lied that I had used it and apologized to her just so I can be rid of her. I think she used to enjoy my apologies as she would smile seductively saying that she had accepted them for a wrong I did not commit! Then, she started dressing more flamboyantly making sure that she stopped for a few minutes at my door before she walked off to where she was going. Although the temptation was great, I kept my distance from Morenike.

The next week, I was back in Calabar to make a final preparation for my departure for the United States. When Peter Nwankwo saw me, the look on his face was like "I thought you had gone mad or dead". He was amazed to see me, and after a few moments, he asked if I was sick or anything of the sort. I told him that I was in perfectly good health. He smiled in his usual cunning way even as I thought about telling him that what I thought he did in collaboration with the other three lecturers was a 'stab in the back'. I thought the better of that and said nothing to him about the juju spell. I emptied my bookshelf, gathered my manuscripts – mostly unpublished poems and plays, and part of an unfinished novel at the time – *Food for Masquerades*, and left Calabar along with some of my personal belongings. This incident made me "escape" back to the United States in November of that year. At one point, after I had been cured, and my wife came to join me in Lagos, I told her that I would like to apply to the University of Lagos. That was a last ditch attempt to remain in Nigeria. I just wanted to get away from Calabar and their Calabar *juju* so bad. There was no time to go through the process of application and waiting for an answer, besides, I had bought a plane ticket to the United States, and so, I resolved to travel back to the United States.

Chapter 2: (At the Black Repertory Theatre.)

When I arrived at the San Francisco International Airport, everything looked familiar to me. I was back in a place where I had my undergraduate and graduate studies – a place where I lived between 1974 and 1979. I was momentarily happy because my 'escape' from the University of Calabar was complete. I knew that I was back in a good place for arts and culture. But my "escape" was not planned well. I did not plan ahead for accommodation and did not anticipate unemployment and starvation.

Luckily for me, I still had the phone number of Mrs. Nora B. Vaughn, who was the Executive

Director of the Black Repertory Theatre. That theatre was then situated at its old location at 1719 Alcatraz Avenue, Berkeley. She had been a good theatre ally back when I was an undergraduate at the University of California at Berkeley (1974-1976) and had produced my early plays such as *The Father of Secrets, The Creator and the Disrupter, Sure Banker, Polygamy* and *The Graduate Palava*. The plays were produced as showcases under the auspices of the New Arts Experience Program. It was designed so that the audience could comment about a play at the end of the production. This was to help the emerging playwright in the re-writing and/or revision of that play.

She was surprised to hear that I was back in the United States, and she said that the last she heard about me was that I had returned to Nigeria to contribute to the development of the country. I did not know what to say to her, definitely, I could not tell her about the *juju* experience for fear that she might either laugh about it or think that I was superstitious or a coward! One who ran away in the face of adversity? Nora Vaughn was an assertive, kind, and a fastidious African American woman. She was in her sixties and her energy and penchant for the theatre were indomitable. She was very much involved in the theatre when she lived in St. Louis, Missouri, and at the time I thought she had transferred that theatre enthusiasm to the San Francisco Bay area, and to the city of Berkeley where she lived. So, when I called her that I was back in the United States she was happy and asked me to come down to the theatre to see some of their productions. I actually accepted one of such invitations and came to the theatre to see a major production, which was an African American play titled *A Day of*

Absence by Douglas Turner Ward. The play was a snapshot of the lives of African Americans who had refused to perform their usual menial jobs in the society such as cooking, cleaning, babysitting, washing, and gardening. They all agreed to take "the day off" so to speak, and white Americans were "forced" to perform all the menial jobs they were not used to. A particular scene in the play was a white woman and her husband. The white woman was as clueless as to what to do with her crying baby, as their African American maid, was honouring 'the day of absence' and had refused to come to work! The white woman's husband was angry even as the baby was crying and the white woman was running helter-skelter confused about what to do about a baby crying incessantly!

When the play was over, I hung around the theatre waiting to talk to Mrs. Vaughn. Everyone walked past me and into their cars parked on the street outside the theatre. They looked at me as if to say "The play is over won't you go home?" I hung around the theatre even as the very last person walked out of the theatre. Then, there were only three of us in the theatre, Mrs. Vaughn, her doting husband who never left her side, and me. I pretended to be placing the chairs back in their proper positions and generally straightening things up, a chore that had already been done by the theatre volunteers! Then Mrs. Vaughn called me in her soft, firm almost musical voice. I walked up to her. "We are going home now. I guess I'll see you tomorrow or sometime." I cringed when she said, "we are going home". I knew that it meant she and her husband would be going home, but where would I go I thought. Then a voice in me said, "You better put your shame aside and tell her your problem or you will end up sleeping outside in the cold." I looked at her and her husband as if to say "Both of you should know that I have no place to go, do I really have to say it for you to know?" I watched Mrs. Vaughn chew gum and her husband dangling the keys to their car and their house before me. My heart skipped a beat. If they got up and chaperoned me out I would be in trouble. The dangling keys revealed told me that the man was getting impatient. Roger, her husband, was an introvert, an intensely quiet man who never spoke unless his wife was speaking. Why was he signalling indirectly saying to his wife to "Let us go"? I felt a lump in my throat. It was hot and burning as if I had swallowed hot coffee. I did not know how to tell her that I had no place to sleep. The words just did not come out. I had never been homeless in my life, except briefly, in Lagos when I was in transition to the United States. Momentarily, my spacious three bedrooms flat complete with a study, and a two bedroom Boys' Quarters at the University of Calabar flashed before my eyes. I snapped out of the surreal feeling and mustered up the courage to tell her that I had no place to stay. My hope was that she would offer me a place to stay in her house for all her children were grown and had left home and it was just her and her husband who was nearing seventy at the time, who were living in their large house a mile from the theatre.

Finally, the words came out: "Mrs Vaughn, I am sorry, but I have no place to go" I muttered, looking at her quiet husband whom I thought did not care much about my predicament. "You have no place to go? Why have you not made a solid arrangement about accommodation before coming back to the U.S?" She asked, looking intently into my eyes. I felt as if her gaze was burning holes in my body, so I looked away and fixed my eyes on one of the spots- lights in the theatre. I felt like a child who had committed an offense and was going to suffer the consequence. I did not answer her question. Where would I begin to tell her about Calabar, the tribalists, my encounter with juju spell, the visit to the Ifa priest, my stay at the Thorpe family home, and my eventual hurried flight out of Nigeria? "Well, honey… Dipo says he has no place to go," she addressed her husband who by then was looking away from his wife and me. My heart began to pound harder like that of an athlete who had just finished running a vigorous one- mile. I could hear the archaic refrigerator all the way in the rear of the building clonking annoyingly. The heat from the large space heater in front of us came out in a sporadic burst of hot air. It was getting to be about 10:30 p.m.

 "Well, honey… what you want us to do?" The husband replied in a snappy manner. "Well, I don't know, honey," his wife replied. "There is no room for him in our house."

Roger concluded. I was shocked. I had expected that answer to come from Mrs. Vaughn, in which case I would have pleaded or begged that she let me stay in their house for a few days at least. I was used to dealing with her because of our theatre alliance which dated back to 1979, but I was not very familiar with her husband. He rarely talked to anyone and he often walked around as if he could not talk at all! There was silence. "Well, we ain't gonna just let him sleep outside in the cold. It's bitterly cold out there Roger" Mrs. Vaughn replied her husband in her soft musical voice. I felt a ray of hope; one of them was on my side. Roger looked at me as if to say "So my wife is on your side?" Then he said, "Well then, what we gonna do about this?" Mrs. Vaughn toyed with her handbag for a minute and said: "If he won't mind, he could sleep in the theatre… but there is no heat, no food or drink, and he can't go out after the doors are locked at night". She concluded. Mrs. Vaughn asked me if that was okay with me, and I answered in the affirmative thanking her for her generosity. They left me in the theatre, locked the doors and left.

The Black Repertory Theatre was a mere store front converted into a shoe-string theatre. Mrs. Vaughn wanted to use the theatre as a place where young African American adolescents could direct their positive energy instead of concentrating on gangs, violence, petty larceny, theft, prostitution, alcoholism, and drugs, which often landed these youngsters in trouble with the law. She believed that the theatre could be used to educate and change society, and also in what she often referred to as "the black spirit" – that indomitable spirit she claimed was capable of overcoming adversity.

My stay at the Black Repertory Theatre was a challenge. I had arrived in the United States in November 1984. It was bitterly cold and all I had were clothes that could be regarded as summer clothes since I was coming from Nigeria and from a tropical climate. My first foray was in a second-hand clothing store near what was the North Berkeley Bart Station. I purchased some second-hand winter clothes and jacket with a little of the few dollars I had. The challenge was at night when I had to sleep on the table in the kitchen at the back of the small theatre. I had reconstructed the table into a makeshift bed. I placed some gray blankets on it, and a cushion on it for a pillow. I had retrieved the cushion from a torn sofa which only had three legs, which was in the lobby of the theatre. When one sat on the sofa it would tilt violently to one side throwing the person to the side it had tilted to. Everyone tried to avoid sitting on that particular sofa, and I wondered why the sofa was not thrown out.

 During the day, when the theatre was abuzz with administrative activities such as composing letters to patrons for financial support, making phone calls, and holding meetings, everything seemed fine. It was at night that I experienced the most discomfort. The large heaters turned on during the day to heat up the building would be turned off when everyone left at about 5.p.m (unless of course there was a stage presentation that day). I would then retire to the rear of the theatre where the kitchen was located. I spent the long winter months freezing and with incurable hunger pangs and I watched the few remaining dollars in my pocket dwindle to about two dollars! Then I thought "What is this nightmare? I must get a job, no matter how menial in order to bounce out of the mental and emotional entrapment. I used to depend on the generosity of the theatre workers – the actresses, actors, volunteer stage hands, directors, and the like. I appreciated their generosity, but it seemed to me that I had made a wrong choice by allowing myself to be hounded out of the University of Calabar, where I was a lecturer and where I lived in a four-bedroom apartment complete with two maids.

One night, it must have been a Sunday night, I was particularly disillusioned. I hated Sunday nights because it meant I won't see any of my benefactors until Tuesday. One of the benefactors, Pharellia, who was a strikingly beautiful African American woman, was always kind to me. She was married to Kevin, one of the resident stage directors. She was also the de-facto Secretary of the theatre. She would bring hamburgers, hot dogs, chili, baked pies, cinnamon cookies, oatmeal cookies, pound cake, cheese casserole, and apple cider, and leave them in the theatre saying "This is for Dipo". It was not long before her husband, began to look at me in the most curious way, sometimes avoiding me altogether. I began to see that Pharellia had a certain romantic feeling towards me, but I was not in the mood for that kind of a thing at the time. I was too challenged by my situation, besides, I did not want to encourage her to become romantically linked to me when she was married, and I, of course, was married.

One day, while Pharellia was typing letters to theatre patrons, she held my hand and said that she liked me! I looked at her face. The little sun that was trying to come out of the gray winter sky made her face even more beautiful. Her skin was black and shining. She had the most beautiful, naturally long jet black hair, that it was easy to see that she must have had some American Indian ancestry. I felt a lump in my throat and I was unable to swallow my own saliva. Her beauty rivaled that of a mermaid. I looked at the gap between her front teeth, and found myself unable to speak; I had become mesmerized by her beauty. Then, totally oblivious about how I mustered the courage to ask, I said "You like me? What about your husband?" There was silence. I heard the postman place letters marked 'Black Repertory Theatre' into the mailbox perennially glued to the outside wall of the theatre. As the howling winter wind blew the postman's winter coat here and there, he held on to his helmet, and swung his bag of letters back onto his back, walking away briskly and saying.

"Good afternoon, Ms.
Pharellia."   Then she said
"My husband"?
 She looked at my eyes and smiled.
"I am going to divorce him." She concluded.

That gave me the impression that things were not going well
between them, but then, I thought I should not be involved with her
as she was still married and I was still married. I told her that my
wife was in Nigeria and that she often reminded me over the phone
to be faithful to her. Pharellia had a very intelligent daughter who
was about eight years old at the time. But it was not long before I
found out that she had kicked her husband out of the house and
gained custody of their eight- year- old daughter. Kevin was also a
volunteer at the theatre. He doubled as a theatre director and tutor
of Saturday theatre workshop for teenagers. He worked tirelessly to
make sure that if the theatre had no funding at all from The City of
Berkeley, there must be money for the Teenage Saturday Theatre
Workshop as the program was called. He also became the Director
of the New Arts Experience Program of the theatre.
The interesting thing about the food Pharellia brought to the theatre
was the fact that people would just stroll to the counter top where
they were placed and helped themselves to them, and in a matter of
minutes, the food would have disappeared. It took me a while to
realize that everyone behaved as if they were a member of a
community -The community of the Black Repertory Theatre. To the
volunteers, a black theatre was not just about staging plays, but it
was an institution which must unite the black community. It was a
place for spreading the beauty and dignity of the black race, and a
place to showcase their goodness. These were some of the beliefs of
the Executive director herself. I used to be so angry because
everyone ate the food Pharellia had generously brought for me. I
thought they had plenty to eat in their various homes so why would
they eat the food Pharellia had brought for me saying specifically
that "This is for Dipo?" So, I invented a game. Whenever I saw

people gravitating towards the countertop where the food items were placed, I would walk briskly towards the counter and stand there just so that they would know that I was in the theatre and the food was mine. Unfortunately, they were never intimidated by my presence. They would just walk up to me and say things like "Oh Dipo, how are you? Did you sleep well last night?" How could I have slept well when there were rats scampering around all night long rummaging for food? They would then scoop up huge chunks of the food and pastries and retire into the lobby area to eat them chatting endlessly and laughing heartily. I even remember one of them, John Travis, a big black man who stood well over six feet tall. He was, by day a bus driver for the company known as *AC Transit*, and at night, a volunteer for the theatre. He stood out in my memory, then because of his incredible acting ability. He had played the role of Walter Lee Younger in Lorraine Hansberry's *A Raisin in the Sun*. He, too, would scoop up what I thought was "my food" and retire to the lobby to eat it! The incredible thing about him was that I heard that he won about twenty-five thousand dollars in a lottery, but that he squandered it all gambling!

Monday was a complete day off for everyone in the theatre. It was a day to rest and to strategize for the activities of the week. Usually, the most vibrant days in the theatre were Wednesdays to Sundays. Experimental plays, workshops, and season productions would fall on these days. The weatherman had predicted a dip in the temperature and there was bitter cold accompanied by raging winds.

As Rufus, the man who kept all the keys to the theatre locked the front door, my heart sank. I could not even escape from the building in case of an emergency; say a fire or something of the sort. I looked at the antique refrigerator positioned in a corner of the kitchen which was making this clunking noise, and then, crept down from the top of the flat kitchen table which was my bed and walked up to it. There was a sound coming from the area of the rear door, which was an exit door, and the emergency exit from the theatre. Of course, I dared not touch that door as the alarm would go off and the Berkeley Police, Fire, and Emergency services would arrive in minutes! I reached the refrigerator and opened its door. I was amazed to see a few rancid apples, a jar of mayonnaise that was turning orange – a sign to me that the mayonnaise was beginning to go bad, a jar of ketchup that was unopened, and a jar of mustard that was unopened. I burst out laughing even though I did not know why. Perhaps I should open the ketchup and mustard and begin to eat them, but then, ketchup and mustard were used to garnish foods like hamburger, hot dogs, etc. They were not foods in themselves. Disappointed, I walked back to my makeshift bed on the bare kitchen table, and pulled the long winter coat (used as a costume for stage performances) around me and tried to sleep. I thought if I was able to sleep, then the hunger would go away. I heard my stomach growl. My thoughts began to go to my wife and children in Nigeria. I did not want to think of how they were faring as I was not in a position that fared better.

Then, I heard a sound. The sound was an all too familiar one to me. Two big rats had made the theatre home as well. I was aware of them the first day I slept in the theatre. To me, they looked like husband and wife as they were always following themselves around. I was not ready for their games that night. True to their nature, they were pests. They disturbed my sleep – the only weapon I tried to use to fight hunger. They would crawl into the metal garbage can in the kitchen and knock off its lid in their practiced fashion of rummaging for food in it. Usually, one would crawl into the garbage can first, while the other would stand by it as if on a watch out for humans that would come and disrupt their foray into the garbage can. I spent thirty minutes watching them and getting a little irritated. They found leftovers and some abandoned apple pie and part of a hamburger bun and they were munching away with great relish. I was jealous. I had never been jealous of rats in my life until that night! They were eating and I could not eat. My stomach growled again and I knew that I would not be able to sleep that night. Then I thought "Why wouldn't someone put any food in this refrigerator?" Then another voice in me said "Well, you…

know, it is a theatre, not a home. The refrigerator is for keeping foods and snack for refreshments after a show." I watched the rats for a while as they ate their buffet and trailed back into their hole beneath the floor of the kitchen.

I kept hearing their sound from beneath the kitchen floor. I never knew that rats could be so restless. The sound they made was a cracking, crackling sound that changed to an annoying scratching sound. I got up incensed with the twin emotions of anger and jealousy. I grabbed a big iron rod, which looked like a prop to me as I weaved my way past the costume section, pulled back the costumes on the massive wooden standing rack to see where the annoying rats were hiding. Their sound was getting closer as I approached a big box on the floor of the costume section into which lovely costumes for stage plays had been thrown carelessly. I picked up a costume which looked like what an Overseer might have won on a southern cotton plantation during slavery. I dropped the costume and held the iron rod high over my head. I was determined to kill the two rats. By doing that, I believed that they would not come and disturb my sleep at night nor taunt me with their gross eating of rancid food from the garbage can. Besides, I did not think that it was hygienic for the rats to be living with me. I had learned that rats carried deadly diseases such as rabies. Simply put, rats and human beings should not cohabitate. Then, the incredible thing happened. The crackling, scratching sound subsided. I waited with one foot forward and the other backward, straining my eyes to see in the dim neon light which illuminated the kitchen. If they dared to come out, Wham! The iron rod would come down on their heads or at least on the head of one of them. I would kill that one, and defer the death of the other one till another day. No! I am not going to sleep with those rats running around my makeshift bed. I waited. The sound stopped. I was disappointed. Did they know my plan? Then I knew that I had to wait for them to begin their exasperating noise again as that was the only way to trace them. I heard the musical big clock of the theatre strike two, and the old Negro spiritual *Swing Low, Swing Chariot*.

Momentarily, I thought that the Chariot should swing low to carry me back to Nigeria where at least I would be able to eat! It was two O'clock in the morning, and I was chasing rats that would not let me sleep. Wham! The iron rod came down, but unfortunately, it came down on my big toe! I yelled and threw the rod away and the rats came out of their hole and scampered towards the direction of my makeshift bed. I thought they gloated about my predicament.

While I was still in pain from the impact of the rod on my toe, one of the rats sat on my make shift pillow – the removable cushion from an armchair in the lobby of the theatre! What? So this one is even trying to take over my table-bed? I limped towards the table and tried to hit it with the iron rod I had recovered from where I threw it. One of the legs of the table gave way, and suddenly, I had no table-bed again! In annoyance I went to the costume area, and slept on a pile of winter coats, making sure to make a heap of them so that I would not feel the coldness of the concrete floor on my body. I found a wooly gray winter knit cap, obviously a costume item, and I took it and wore it pulling the entire cap to my mouth to keep out the winter cold. My breath was the only warm thing I could feel, but it was not enough to keep me warm. I realized that the cold, particularly the frosty breeze was coming in from the different cracks in the base of the kitchen area, and from the openings of the doors and windows that were not properly sealed to keep out the cold. I saw an old copy of *Ebony Magazine* and picked it up trying to read about the huge financial success of the Johnson Family Beauty Products in Chicago. I really could not read as the neon light was really too dim. Minutes later, I fell asleep.

I was beginning to suffer from cabin fever. How could I be holed up in a theatre for two days? I found some stale crackers in an abandoned cabinet and grabbed them. It was about eight O'clock in the morning. Crackers for breakfast, I thought. They were about six small packets in all. My favourite breakfast meal when I was a student at the University of California at Berkeley was pancakes with eggs and sausage which I usually bought at the MacDonald's restaurant. At that moment, I craved that breakfast, but I knew that there was really a fat chance of me getting anything of the sort at that particular moment. I wanted coffee with milk and sugar so badly. That would have numbed the taste of the stale crackers. I looked out of the front window of the theatre. I could see cars going up and down Alcatraz Avenue. There was a woman who was pushing along a shopping cart full of bags. She was the type we usually referred to as a "bag lady". Bag ladies were homeless women who slept under bridges, flyovers, bus stations, and train stations. They usually "live' out of the perennial bags they haul along. For a moment, I thought perhaps I was a "bag man" of some sorts, but that, the difference between the "bag lady" and me was the fact that I was holed up in the theatre and not moving from place to place.

Suddenly, there was Hare Krishna music! A group of Hare Krishna devotees emerged on the road and were going in a procession towards the North Berkeley Bart Station. They were all dressed in their trademark pink attire which looked in part like South East Asian Saris and with cylindrical drums hung across their shoulders which they played with great dexterity. The infectious rhythm of the drums became louder and that drew my attention to the front window by the entrance to the theatre. Of course, the door was locked so I could only look at them through the window. *"Hare Krishna, Krishna Krishna, Hare, Hare, Hare Hare, Hare,"* I heard them chant incessantly. Some Berkeley women had joined the procession. They were white women, and they were swaying vigorously to the rhythm of the drums. One of them, a very tall woman, was acting possessed, even as the drumming became louder and sweat was dripping from the brow of the drummers. It was amazing to see the devotees scantily clad in such winter conditions. I was not sure how their partly exposed bodies such as shoulder, stomach, and part of their backs, could tolerate the bitter cold. Perhaps the drumming and dancing kept them warm. They got to the front of the theatre and stopped. They were playing the drums vigorously as ever and gyrating. The tiny bells they held with two or three fingers from each hand were sounding incessant and seemed to serve as accentuation to the drumming. The tall woman removed a flimsy scarf she had tied around her neck and was twirling around like a whirlwind. Then, she jumped up and down vigorously, with her breasts bouncing up and down uncontrollably. A short Hare Krishna devotee got in front of her and began to play vigorously. As if that was her cue, another woman got in front of the tall dancer and began to dance in front of her. It was as if the second woman was saying "You can't be the only center of attraction, I have to be noticed too". Some passers-by stopped to watch them. Even a jogging fanatic with a very long blond beard, which made him look like Charleton Heston playing Moses, in *The Ten Commandments,* stopped. He then began to jog in one spot and was watching the Hare Krishna group. The jogger, a health fanatic, lived around the corner from the theatre. He went jogging every day making sure that he jogged on Alcatraz Avenue, where the theatre was located. I watched the jogger in his red jogging suit and a red bandanna with a pair of red tennis shoes to match. His pair of socks was white with red trimmings. Jogging in place was his dance to the Hare Krishna rhythm. Not long after that an old man on a bicycle got off his bike and stopped to watch the group. He leaned on his bike and began to clap to the rhythm of the drums. Not long after the man on the bike arrived, the Hare Krishna group continued their procession towards the Bart station.

I went back to the kitchen. When I got there, I scrutinized the crackers to make sure that my friends, the rats, had not eaten any part of them! I was already salivating just looking at the crackers. Then, I checked to make sure that the wraps were not broken, and that there was no nibble mark on the crackers. If the wraps were broken, and there were nibbling marks around the edges of the crackers, that would indicate that the rats had gotten to them before me. Luckily for me, the wraps were intact. Yet, I was afraid to break them open and eat them. There was nothing fancy about the crackers. They were ordinary crackers people throw into their clam chowder soups to thicken them up at a restaurant in the Berkeley

Marina. The wraps even had the name of the restaurant on them –
The Berkeley Marina Restaurant and Seafood. I ate the crackers
and went to the faucet in the kitchen to drink some cold water. The
water was particularly cold as the hot water section of the kitchen
faucet was not working. I felt good somewhat – I had beaten the
rats to the crackers.

I had been in negotiation with the Executive Director of the
theatre, for the production of my play – *The Father of Secrets*. It
was going to be a revival of some sorts as the play had been
produced in the theatre many years back. It was to be performed
under their New Arts Experience Program. Kevin, the estranged
husband of Pharellia was chosen to direct the play, but he opted out
at the last minute saying he was too busy with his job during the
day and he would be unable to direct it. I thought perhaps he had a
grudge with me because Pharellia was always saying to everyone
"This is for Dipo". Perhaps he was suffering from an unwarranted
jealousy? The New Arts Experience Program was an experimental
program which showcased the works of new playwrights. At the
end of the performance, the audience would be asked to wait behind
and ask questions about the play, and the production.

Mrs. Vaughn arranged for a new Director for the play. He was
Steven Jones a perennially jovial man who was happy to be
directing what he called "an African play". I did not want to be
drawn into the intricacies of the rehearsal and the eventual stage
production. To me, that was tantamount to constituting an
impediment to a woman who was in labour. Steve asked me too
many questions. Some of the questions were: "What was life in
Africa like? What is the meaning of Ifa? How does an Ifa Priest
consult the oracle? Do people really believe in Ifa? What about
patriarchy? How does patriarchy affect Yoruba Traditional
Religion?" I wanted him to apply himself and bring out whatever
meaning the play yielded.
He got a copy of the play from me and took it home to read.

The next day he came to the theatre asking me the meaning of
the numerous Yoruba words in the play. I obliged him on that score

by telling him the meaning of the Yoruba words, but then, he asked me if I knew anyone who could play the title role of *The Father of Secrets*. I told him that I did not know anyone who could play the role and that he should just follow his audition plans, and make his casting choice after the audition. I knew the problem. The play's action centers on the lead character. If the lead character fails, the play fails, simple. Steve Jones was brilliant enough to know this and I was secretly glad about that, but I did not tell him about it. "I still want an African to play the lead role," he said to me during one of his auditions for the play. "Do you know any African who could play this role?" I told him that I did not. As far as I was concerned, drama was a lone profession in those days, and there were not many Nigerians, nor Africans who were in that field of study in the entire San Francisco Bay Area. I was the only Nigerian and the only African who studied drama at the University of California at Berkeley throughout my undergraduate years! I used to dodge him whenever I saw his light blue Chevrolet Malibu parked in front of the theatre. I would know that he had rehearsals that evening.

One evening I saw him alight from the car with another man. I was curious. He never gave anyone a lift in his car and the car was always clean, neat, and free of mechanical defects. I stood at a comfortable distance, watching him and the man talking and gesturing. My curiosity grew. When he entered the theatre, he asked me if I knew the man he had brought to the theatre. I told him I did not, and then he said to me "This is Dr. Sam Oni. He is an instructor at Laney College in Oakland. He is a Yoruba man, but was raised in Ghana as his parents were traders in that country. He speaks some Ghanaian languages – Twi, and Ewe. He is not very fluent in Yoruba but he understands the Yoruba language very well. He would be able to handle the Yoruba nuances and idioms of the play and the incantations. I think he can play the role of *The Father of Secrets*."

Dr. Sam Oni and I exchanged pleasantries and I was amazed as to how Steve found Sam. It was later on, that Sam invited me to his house in Oakland which was very tastefully furnished. He was gainfully employed as an Instructor at Laney College, Oakland, apparently financially secure, and living in his own plush three bedroom apartment. Instantly, I knew that this man was not competing for food with rats! He had a Ph.D., but it was not in theatre or any of its related disciplines. He was not married at the time, and I was surprised to see that he was living in a three bedroom apartment all by himself! I was so impressed by the man's uncanny ability to learn his lines and to remember them. He was such a descent and a humble man, and anytime I was invited to his house I would make sure to fill up my belly so that I won't have to worry about food when I got back to the theatre!

One Saturday afternoon, he invited me to what he called "Saturday Afternoon Barbecue". He had these "Saturday Afternoon Barbecues" at least once a month! I ate so much baby back ribs, steaks, hamburgers, hot dogs, and Polish kielbasa with sauerkraut that I only stopped when I thought I was going to be sick in my stomach! Of course, he found me curled up in a corner of his second living room listening to reggae music. He asked me why I had not eaten anything! I told him that I had eaten a lot, and all I wanted at that time was my favourite red wine, *Mateus Rose*. Experience told me that if I had eaten too much, all I had to do was to drink some red wine, and it would aid my digestion and my stomach would feel light again. Instantly, he disappeared and reappeared with two more bottles of chilled *Mateus Rose*, placed them in front of me and disappeared to go and chat with guests from Laney College who were standing on his patio, drinking, chatting, and laughing. One of the guests, apparently drunk, was singing the *Star-Spangled Banner* off key of course!

A very beautiful white woman, Mary Dobson, kept dragging him all over the place, and occasionally, trying to kiss him. She dragged him into the second living room where I was curled up sipping my wine, trying to kiss him in front of me. She also tried to get Sam to dance with her. He seemed reluctant. She ignored his reluctance and danced on her own, and a bit out of rhythm to the reggae songs of Bob Marley such as: *"No Woman No Cry", "Lively*

Up Yourself", *"Get Up Stand Up"*, and *"Them Belly Full But We Hungry"*. These tunes were playing on the record player. The last tune, *"Them Belly Full But We Hungry"* reminded me of the African proverb "An old woman is always uneasy when dry bones are mentioned." I felt odd. How could I be listening to a tune like that when in fact I was "hungry" at the theatre! I was in a world of my own. I loved reggae music and to this day I still do. I ignored the beautiful brunette woman who was trying to seduce Sam, and who was now dancing seductively in front of me and continued to listen to the music and to sip my wine.

Then, the incredible thing happened. She grabbed my hand and pulled me up from where I was sitting, and asked me to dance with her! I pleaded with her to let me put my glass of wine down, but she said I should just hold the glass in my hand and dance with her! I felt trapped. What if Sam came back from the patio where he was chatting with his friends to find out that I was dancing with his girlfriend in his own living room at a Saturday Afternoon Barbecue party he had invited me to? What if Sam thought I was trying to seduce his girlfriend? I protested vehemently, but she held on to my hand. I did not know where she got the energy to hold on to me so tightly. I could smell her lovely fragrance and I felt the warmth of her very soft hands. Looking at her sleepy, romantic eyes, I thought in my mind, if that was a trap, it would not work. Then she said: "I know what you are thinking... look, Sam wouldn't mind. He is a very nice guy". I turned her words over in my mind "He is a very nice guy". Well, I knew that Sam was a very nice guy, perhaps everyone knew that Sam was a very nice guy, but he would not be so nice if he thought I was trying to seduce his girlfriend. She drew me closer to her and her whole body was now next to mine. I was aroused, but I pretended that I was not.

We began a kind of slow dance which was totally out of sync with Bob Marley's reggae music. I felt her warm, voluptuous breasts pressing against my chest and I began a conscious effort not to enjoy it, not to be aroused. I only knew I had failed in that attempt when she said something like "Whow! What do we have here?" Moments later she said," It's big and strong; I can feel it." I did not answer her. I was highly disappointed that she has felt it! She made an attempt to touch it, but I pulled my knees together and her hands landed on my thigh. "Oh! Come on," she said. I shook my head in the negative. I understood her intentions perfectly. "Oh! Don't be a party pooper" she said, smiling. "Look, everyone is having fun here… you can even hear someone singing *The Star Spangled Banner* isn't that lovely and patriotic?" She concluded, smiling seductively. Although she had been drinking, I could not discern if she was tipsy, drunk or both. She drank Heinekens, and occasionally, she would change to vodka. We were close enough for me to smell her beer breath competing with her romantic perfume. Then she placed her head on my shoulder moving my body here and there, and I merely followed her sheepishly around the living room. I felt like a mannequin in her hand. Perhaps I should tell her that I wanted to go and urinate or something – anything to do to get away from her seemed an attractive option to the pending entrapment. "I hear you are a playwright and Sam says he is going to be in your play. That's lovely you know. Sam talks a lot about you," she said, rubbing her nose against mine! Again, I felt her beer breath. I turned her words over in my mind. "Sam talks a lot about you?" Why would Sam be talking about me to his girlfriend? Surely, he must have something more important to say to her than to talk about me. "I am Mary Dobson. Sam and I teach at Laney College in Oakland." She continued. "I am Dipo Kalejaiye," I said, even as I felt her breathing on my neck. "I used to teach at the University of Calabar in Nigeria". I. said. "Yes, yes, Dipo from Nigeria right?" I replied in the affirmative. "Have you ever heard of a Nigerian playwright named Wole Soyinka?" She asked as she twirled me around a couple of times. "Yes, I replied". "Well, I teach one of his plays in my English class at Laney… *The Lion and the Jewel.* Do you know his play *The Lion and the Jewel*?" I told her that I knew the play and had read it. Then, she smiled and said, "Good, maybe you can come and talk to some of the students in my Third World Literature Class about *The Lion and the Jewel.*"

There was silence. Then she asked: "Is polygamy very common in Nigeria?" I answered that some people definitely practiced it. She kept trying to touch it, and I kept trying to keep my knees together. Now, I was like a sleepwalker hunched over and moving around the big living room. I was resolved not to open my knees for her to reach the object of her desire. I wanted someone to walk into the living room, that way, the privacy we enjoyed would disappear like soap bubbles and I would break away from her firm grip. Luckily for me, Sam entered and saw us. He smiled and said something like "Oh Mary, there you are. I was looking for you everywhere." I felt like Judas and I broke away from her grip instantly. "Well, you wouldn't dance with me, and Dipo here agreed to dance with me". I caught her last sentence… "Dipo here agreed to dance with me". I never agreed to dance with her! Then John said "Okay, okay, you can dance with Dipo no problem, it is just that everyone is asking for you to come and sing acapella for them" She replied John by saying "Just tell them I'll be there when I finish dancing with Dipo!" I resented the fact that John did not just drag her off to go and sing for the multitude on the patio. "You see, I love singing. I am an opera singer you know. Do you know the opera *The Marriage of Figaro* by Wolfgang Amadeus Mozart? I loved that opera. Look, singing is my hobby… particularly a cappella singing. One day, perhaps when I retire from Laney College, I want to go to Europe, to sing in the great opera houses of Europe. You know – The Teatro DI San Carlo in Italy, or The GranTeatro Del Liceu in Spain. You know, I have a piano at home. Do you play the piano?" I answered that I only play the piano by ear as I could not read musical notations. Not long after Sam left the living room, Mary disentangled herself from me and went to sing for guests on the patio. I could hear her wonderful and mesmerizing operatic voice singing the part of Susanna in Mozart's *The Marriage of Figaro.*

After a while, I began to decline Sam's invitation to come to his house. I wanted to stop being a parasite! I was beginning to be ashamed of eating in his house. I thought I had brought great shame on myself and I had better snap out of my Bohemian lifestyle and live a conventional one like him. My hunger pangs at the Black Repertory Theatre came back, yet I did not go to Dr. Sam Oni's house again. He thought he had offended me in some way, but I told him that he had not offended me at all. He did not accept my explanation and I felt really bad. He was so decent, kind, gainfully employed, financially stable and living a conventional life I could only dream about at the time. He told me that he thought I was very talented and that he had read the play, *The Father of Secrets* and that he thought it was very good.

Surprisingly, he mentioned that he had read somewhere that the play had been awarded a First Prize in the *James. D. Phelan Literary Award in Playwriting*. I merely looked at him in the most curious way and nodded in the affirmative. I was not going to let him convince me to start coming to his house again because he thought I was "talented". I felt like a failure compared to him and I began to count how many days to the opening and eventual closing of my play at the theatre so that I won't have to see him again. Not that he had done anything wrong to me, but so that he would not have to invite me to his house. I really wanted him to discriminate against me because of my Bohemian lifestyle, but he refused to do that instead, he tried to court my friendship. The more I resisted, the more he tried! The ironic part of all of these was the fact that Sam felt "honoured" to be associated with me and I felt hopeless and inadequate.

The rehearsals began in earnest. There was the need for publicity. Pharellia had contacted the usual theatre patrons in the area, who donated modestly towards the project. The theatre arranged for the printing of posters and flyers. They were nothing flamboyant, just practical. They carried the essential information about the play that a prospective member of the audience needed to know. The rehearsals were on Wednesday evenings.

One day, a car pulled up to the theatre and a white woman got out and entered the theatre. Immediately she entered I recognized her. Her name was Marianne Lawson She was my ex-girlfriend up until 1979 when I left the United States. I had left the United States without telling her, and had been gone for five years! I first met her at *Ashkenaz* a night club on San Pablo Avenue in Albany sometime in 1977. I had gone there to listen to the music of a Ghanaian band known as *Hedzolleh Soundz*. The nightclub was very popular, attracting musicians from the United States and some parts of the world. There were Flamenco music and dance, Cajun/ Zydeco Music, West African Highlife, Brazilian Samba, Salsa, Blue Grass, and Tango, just to name a few. With *Ashkenaz*, at that time, Berkeley was truly experiencing a musical Renaissance. *Ashkenaz* was truly a famous hot spot for an enriching musical experience. It was always crawling with music and dance enthusiasts to the extent that occasionally, overcrowding occurs, and some people had to listen to the enchanting music standing outside! The dance floor was like choice meat among starving lions. As soon as the music began, there was a maddening rush for the dance floor that I had never seen in my life. The members of *Hedzolleh Soundz* had made the Berkeley area home, and they had played with the South African trumpeter and Musician – Hugh Masekela

"I heard you were back," she said, holding my hand and dragging me to the place where the rehearsal was taking place. "How did you know that I was back in the United States?" I asked. "Someone told me you know… someone at the *Berkeley Flea Market*. She said she was your classmate at the University of California at Berkeley and that she saw the flyer for your play at the Saturday Berkeley Flea Market and she just guessed that perhaps you were back. She was right." She hugged me and said that she was happy to see me. She wanted me to watch the rehearsal of the play, but I was reluctant as that seemed to me like tasting the stew before it was done. When she insisted, I followed her to watch Sam Oni struggle with the Yoruba words in the first scene of the play. I winced where I stood, leaning against the wall, and then walked up to Steven to tell him the correct pronunciation of the Yoruba word - "*egbe*" which meant juju medicine for disappearing. Sam had pronounced it wrong by using the wrong intonation. That made the word sound like the name of a tribe in Ilorin, Nigeria! Marianne was still standing by my side and smiling. We continued to watch the rehearsals for a while, but knowing my nature, rehearsals bore me unless I was the one directing the play. I told her so and that I did not want to watch the rehearsals anymore. We walked away from it and towards the lobby of the theatre. Then we sat down. "Is it good the way you disappeared and you didn't let me know?" She asked. I looked at her for a minute and wondered why after five years she was asking me that kind of question. I kept quiet. "I always think about you," she said, looking at me intently. I was not happy to hear that as I thought that if a man walked away from a woman's life for five years, that woman should have moved on with her life. I told her that I was married and that my wife would soon join me in the United States, although I knew that would not happen for about a year and a half.

The rehearsal ended at about 9.p.m. As usual, Rufus would lock up the theatre at exactly ten. Marianne hung around with me and kept following me all around. I bid Sam goodbye, and waved at Mary Dobson, his opera singer girlfriend. I saw her dragging him along to the place where his Mercedes Benz car was parked. They entered the car and drove off. It was interesting to note that Mary Dobson tried not to be as friendly with me even when she had come to the theatre where my play was being rehearsed for a production. Perhaps she was "jealous" of the white girl she saw holding my hand – my ex-girlfriend Marianne Lawson. To my surprise, Marianne asked me where I was staying. I did not want to tell her that I was sleeping in the theatre. "Really, Dipo, where do you stay?" She asked again, apparently insisting on an answer. I thought the question was suspicious. Perhaps someone had told her that I was sleeping in the theatre? But who cares so much about me to be peddling that kind of information? "Well, I have no place to stay, so I am sleeping in the theatre" I finally answered her. "In the theatre, honestly, Dipo… but why are you sleeping in the theatre? It must be awfully cold in there at night," she replied. I told her that I knew it was always cold in the theatre at night, but that was the only choice I had at that time. Then she said I must come and live with her, at least temporarily until I can get a place of my own. I thought about the offer and tried to refuse it. How could I be living with an ex-girlfriend, I abandoned for five years, and I had become a married man? When I thought about the option – heat, and food, I agreed to live with her in her two - bedroom apartment very near the grocery store known as *Safeway*. Actually, her apartment was not very far from the theatre. That evening, I told Mrs. Vaughn that I was leaving the theatre. She seemed surprised, but relieved that I was getting away from the challenges of staying in a place without heat or food in the middle of winter.

Marianne and I got into her car and she drove towards her apartment chatting with me all the way and trying to catch up with me about old times. We even reminisced about how I met her at *Ashkenaz*. "You were sitting on my chair, and when I came back from the restroom, the music was loud, electrifying, and the dance floor accommodated a sea of people. I was surprised to see you sitting in my chair. Didn't you see my coat on the chair?" I answered that I did not notice it at all. She laughed and said " I took one look at you, decided that you were handsome and you better just sit on my chair while I grabbed another and placed it next to you," I told her that I remembered that incident very well. Then she stopped the car abruptly in front of what looked like an apartment complex. "Wait just a minute here I will be right back," she said as she jumped out of her car. The engine was running so I turned up the heat in the car it was getting really cold and my ears were freezing. Perhaps the heater was not performing at its optimum. Moments later, she returned with a boy of about six years old. The boy was obviously the result of a union between a white person and a black person. He had golden brown hair, which was curly and long, reaching down to his shoulders. His eyes looked bluish green to me and they had this intelligent, inquisitive sparkle in them. He seemed very animated and vocal. "Mum who is this?" He asked. Marianne looked at me, and said: "Jason, say hello to Dipo." The boy looked at me, squinted behind what looked like an oversized pair of eyeglasses, and said "Hello Dipo". She drove for about a mile or two and spoke casually; "Dipo, this is my son, Jason" I looked at her and told her that I did not know that she had a son. She joked that five years was long enough for a person to have a son. "You have been gone for five years Dipo, a lot can happen in five years, you know," she continued as she swerved into a corner street and said we would be in her apartment in minutes. "Mum, I am hungry" Jason cut in. "Just wait till we get home okay." But Jason would have none of that and he pestered Marianne even more about the fact that he was hungry. "Mum, I want pizza and ice cream." He said. But Marianne insisted that when he got home, he could have chicken, broccoli, and some macaroni and cheese. "I don't want chicken and broccoli Mum, and you know I hate broccoli" Marianne then told him that it was chicken, broccoli, and macaroni and cheese, or nothing. Then she turned to me and spoke as if delivering a lecture:

Dipo, it was when you stopped coming to Ashkenaz that I met his dad. We became friends, he is from Jamaica, his name is Trevor Williams, but everyone called him "Jahman." He was a member of a Jamaican Reggae group, Light of Zion, the one you composed some lyrics for… you remember that don't you Babylon Reggae or something? I nodded in the affirmative. They were singing that after you had left for Nigeria. Whenever they sang that song, it made me think of you, and I wondered why you disappeared like that without even telling me. Did you hate me that much? Anyway, I went to hear Light of Zion play at Ashkenaz one night. After the group's performance, he struck up a conversation with me. He was cool and mellow then. His eyes had this melting hypnotic influence on me; it glowed and sparkled like diamonds in the dark. After the show, he kept following me around and even into the parking lot where I parked my car. He just kept on talking to me; he was going to talk my ears off, and it was cold outside. I asked him to come into the car, and I started the engine, just so that I can turn on the heater. When the inside of the car was warm enough, I told him I had to go, but he wouldn't even get out of the car! He leaned back, brought out a roll of marijuana, and began to smoke it coolly, asking me if I wanted to take a puff. I told him "No". I had only tried marijuana once, it made me dizzy, and so I vowed never to touch it again. Finally, I invited him home for some drinks… you know… just-drinks and a conversation under some romantic lighting. We talked until about two O'clock in the morning. He told me it was too late for him to go home. At first, I insisted that he had to go home as I was not interested in a "one night stand", but he pleaded with me saying that if I pushed him out into the cold he would have to walk home. He told me that I was beautiful. Before I knew it, he had brought out some red, gold, and green candles. He lit them and looked at me with those hypnotic diamond eyes, so I took pity on him, but I told him he had to sleep on the sofa in the living room, even as he held me so close and we danced slowly to the music that was obviously fast. He agreed to sleep in the living room, but when the lights were out in my room, I felt his large warm hands under my blanket. It was a cold night, his hands felt good on my body. He told me that he was a Rastafarian. That he had lost his mother when he was only seven years old, and that it was his grandmother who raised him, and that his dad was a drunk who used to beat his mum a lot, and that one day he just packed up and left the house. No one ever saw him again. Trevor was mellow and cool then, not this kind of wild animal he has now become. Well, I think I have said enough, Jason is in the car. She concluded.

I was surprised to hear that Marianne had a long custody battle with Trevor (or Jahman) which involved long proceedings in a court which had jurisdiction over child custody cases.
She made a case against Trevor, saying that he was a musician who traveled a lot, a lead singer for that matter and that Jason's best interest would not be served by being itinerant with his dad. That

the child needed a parent, who lived in one place, had an apartment, a regular job, and a regular income. That way, the child would have stability and his education would not be adversely affected. She said:

Trevor fought the court's decision and lost. Can you imagine Trevor telling me that he wanted to take my own son to Jamaica? He wanted to take my son to be raised in Jamaica for what? I couldn't agree with him on that. He was not paying any child support anyway. He even made matters worse when he said his mother was dead, and that his grandmother would be taking care of Jason. His grandmother indeed; I could not agree with him on that. I don't like him anymore. He has a temper, and he does not listen. He lacks understanding, and when he is upset, he can be like a lion tearing up a gazelle for lunch in the African jungle. He can be a real monster. I just hope Jason does not take after him. She concluded.

Later, she drove into her parking spot under the apartment complex. "Mum, is Dipo is going to be your friend? Jason asked, holding his mother's hand, and still whining about wanting to eat pizza. Marianne laughed and said, "Dipo is always my friend". The boy was silent as we climbed the stairs to the second floor of the apartment complex. "Mum, does my dad know about Dipo?" The boy asked again. "No, honey, but I am going to tell your dad about him". The boy was quiet again. Marianne opened the door into her two bedroom apartment. "Mom, do you like Dipo more than my dad?" The boy asked again. "Honey, you are asking too many questions. Here, let me help you take off your winter coat, and you get to hang it up in your room." But the boy said, "Oh mum please hang it up for me". Marianne replied that the rule in the house was for the boy to hang up his clothes himself.
It was early December of 1984 when I began to live with Marianne. It was the thick of winter, but I was not as cold as I used to get sleeping on the "table-bed" I had invented at the Black Repertory

Theatre a month earlier. Ironically, Marianne hated the heat, even though the heater in her apartment worked perfectly. She said it gave her a headache. When it is turned on, it is like a real fiery furnace. Marianne and I had an agreement. I was to babysit Jason when she went to work, or she stepped out to go the grocery store or to run errands. I was not to let him go out under any circumstance, and I was not to open the door for "Jahman". She said she did not trust him and that he might come to forcibly take the boy to Jamaica when she was not around. I was comfortable in Marianne's house for a while, but I did not like the babysitting part of the deal. Jason became rambunctious. I could not control him when his mother was not at home. He would insist that I play with him, bringing out what seemed like an endless array of toys he wanted us to play with. I tried to oblige him a few times, but I got no credit for that. To top that off, he would want me to watch television with me. Most of the time he would want me to watch cartoons and children's programs with him. Disney programs were his favourite. At first, I would pretend that I was enjoying the program by laughing and rolling on the floor with him, but it was not long before I had to admit that I was not enjoying it. By doing this, I hurt his feelings and he was not happy. He would 'threaten' to report me to his mother. I think intrinsically, he knew that I was at the mercy of his mum and that he would, as young as he was then, try to blackmail me!

He would 'report' me to his mum saying things like "Mum, Dipo is no fun. He wouldn't play with me. He wouldn't watch *Tom and Jerry* with me, I want my dad". Sometimes, it would be the cartoon – *Mickey Mouse,* that would catch his fancy, and he would complain about me to his mother as before saying "Mum. Dipo won't watch *Mickey Mouse* with me." It became a running game. He would want to watch a cartoon and I was required to watch the cartoon with him. I was not sure whether it was because of this issue that he said to his mother one day, "I want my dad". Marianne replied by saying that Jason knew the routine about his dad and that his dad would come when he was required, according to the court, to come and visit him. Of course, he was always asking for his dad, and this made his mum quite angry. The anger was precipitated by the boy's nagging and Jahman's ineptitude as a father.

I got to find out one strict rule about Marianne; she made up her mind never to have sex with any man, even Jason's dad, inside that apartment. I guessed that was her way of keeping her integrity intact and bringing Jason up as a single mother who was not showing a child such an inappropriate adult behaviour. She told me that she loved Jason very much and she wanted the best for him and that was why she took that decision. She never asked me for sex, and we were never romantically linked in any way. She made me understand that she brought me into the apartment because we had been good friends before and that the issue of sex was out of it. The day she told me about that I was mortified somewhat, not because I wanted sex with her, but because I did not have such an intention in mind anyway. The nature of the problems I had was so overwhelming that I never thought of something of that nature, in essence, at that time at least, I did not care for that. So, to me, it was as if she was warning me about something I never had the intention of doing. When I met her at *Ashkenaz,* five years back, she was 'freer and more liberal' in behaviour, perhaps at that time, she was younger and single. After she gave birth to Jason, it seemed that she became a bit subdued, stricter and more orthodox. Even with her son, she was conventional and strict. The example I gave earlier came to my mind. She considered pizza 'junk food' and would not allow her son to eat it, insisting instead, on the more nutritious chicken, broccoli, and macaroni and cheese.

Throughout my stay with her, I never saw another man in her apartment or her bedroom. I slept in the living room most of the time, as the only other bedroom was for Jason. Her bedroom was a 'no-go' area for me.

One day, I believe it was a Saturday evening; Marianne and I were watching television. What was on television was not really that exciting, perhaps, an old rerun of some situation comedy or something of that nature. Later, I convinced her that we should watch one of my favourite movie actors – Clint Eastwood in what was known as a 'Spaghetti Western' – *Two Mules for Sister Sarah*. Jason had just come in from outside where he was playing with some of his friends. Marianne changed the channel because she did not want her son watching the violence in the movie. He was only allowed outside to play with his friends if his mother was at home. Perhaps he did not lock the door when he came in, but suddenly, a huge man with dreadlocks, which came down to his neck and shoulders burst in smoking marijuana! He must have been lurking around the playground watching his son play with other boys in the apartment building. Perhaps he trailed him unnoticed to Marianne's apartment. Marianne was startled. She composed herself and got up. I was amazed at the sheer size of the man whose chest was so broad I thought one could place a huge mortar and pestle on it, pound yam vigorously, and he would feel no pain! He looked like he must have been about six feet two inches. The smoke from the marijuana had formed a dense fog in the living room. For a minute or so, the smoke prevented me from seeing his face. Jason began to cough and to fan the smoke away from his face with his sweatshirt. Marianne was visibly angry; apparently, one thing she could not tolerate was the sight of Jahman smoking marijuana before Jason. Instinctively, Jahman seemed to realize that fact, and he put out the marijuana with an index finger and a thumb and put it into the front pocket of the green army fatigue sort of trench coat he was wearing. He also wore a pair of combat boots. He smiled. I was shocked that such a rough and tumble man could have a disarming smile. Perhaps he was showing off to his son I thought. "Jahman, you can't just walk in here like that uninvited. We had an agreement. When you want to see your son you call me first." Marianne spoke in annoyance.

"Yeah man. I ain't gonna be calling you nothing when Ah wanna to see my son" Jahman replied. Jason ran up to him and he picked him up and gave him a few rubs with his large hands on his brown curly hair. "How is my man doing?" He asked. "I am a fine dad, only that

I have missed you too much." Jahman replied that he missed his son too. All this time, Marianne was incensed and trying to control herself. "So you've been hiding around my apartment building?" Jahman insisted that he must see his son whenever he wanted with Marianne threatening to go back to the court and ask the judge to cancel Jahman's visitation rights. "Yeah man… So, this is the African you've been doing it with?" Jahman asked sarcastically. "Look Jahman, I have not been doing it with any African, or anybody for that matter, and even if I have been doing it with him why is it your concern? You told me you were married to a Jamaican woman, so what do you care?" Marianne concluded still fuming with anger and pacing up and down the living room. "Yeah man, I'm married to some Jamaican woman who cooks fried catfish, red beans and rice, and collard greens for me all the time." I heard Jason say something to his dad, and then Marianne cut in "Well then, why don't you go to your Jamaican woman and leave me alone?" Jahman let out a loud guttural laughter. "Ah Marianne, you have my son, man; and I want my son man, " he said even as he sat down on one of the two sofas in the living room, with his son on his lap. "Jason needs to take a bath and get ready for dinner," Marianne said, hoping that the announcement would bring his impromptu visit to an abrupt end. "Hey, I come to see my son man, and he going nowhere man" Jahman retorted. There was an argument about the fact that Jahman was not paying the court ordered monthly child support. He argued that he had not been getting a lot of gigs and therefore had no money, that he was in the studio trying to record an album which he hoped would bring in some money. Marianne was not impressed, and she asked him whether their son would have to wait till he released his album and received his royalty before Jason could be fed, clothed, and educated. He shouted at the top of his voice that Marianne should be quiet because she did not understand the ways of an artist. She got angry and called him a "starving artist."
They argued for a while and I had to leave the apartment temporarily in order for them to sort out their differences.

Suddenly, I heard a huge commotion coming from the apartment, Marianne was shouting and screaming, and Jason was saying "Please dad, don't beat up my mum… please daddy." I could hear the boy crying and Jahman's booming voice overshadowing everything. I ran back inside. I did not want to be someone who deserted Marianne at her time of need. I thought about calling the police, but thought the better of that.

I knew from my knowledge about Rastafarians that they hated the police with a passion. Momentarily, the song *I shot the Sheriff* by Bob Marley came to my mind. What if the police came and Jahman shot him? Then, there would have been a lot of trouble, perhaps, more than the issue of domestic violence or girlfriend battering that was at hand. There would have been a murder case to contend with, and I would have been called up as a witness.

When I got back inside, I was surprised to see Marianne in the middle of the sitting room with pinkish red bruises on her cheek, arms, neck, and face. Jahman was standing over her panting like a lion in the wilderness after killing an antelope. His eyes were two red lights flashing endlessly. Marianne was curled up on the floor like a snake, and Jahman had her in a kind of choke hold. I went to him and tried to disentangle his hand from her neck. "What you want African man?" He asked, in his thick Jamaican accent, and his eyes still flashing as before. I felt his heavy breathing and the smell of marijuana that was coming out of his nostril. He struggled with me, and I felt inadequate against his massive strength, but I persisted in my effort to disentangle his hand from Marianne's neck. I begged him to please leave her alone and that he was such a tall hefty man and Marianne was a mere five feet four inches, and that it was not fair for him to be battering her. "I say what you want African man?" He asked again, but I begged him as before to please just leave her alone, at least because of his son. I tried to tell him that he can't just beat up someone who was taking care of his son when he was on his many musical tours. He looked at me and then asked me if I knew that Rastafarians originated from Africa, from the lineage of the late Emperor Haile Selassie of Ethiopia. I told him that I was aware of that history. He asked me if I knew what his nickname – "Jahman" meant. I told him that I did not, and then he said it meant "Man of God". He said the word "Jah" meant God. I told him that there was nothing godly about what he had just done to Marianne. Then he asked me if I knew that humans originated from Africa. I told him that I have read that in history and anthropological books. He also asked if I knew anything about Dr. L. S. B. Leaky, and he told me that his research had concluded that humans originated from Africa. He said that one line from Fela Ransome- Kuti's song asserted that "Africa was the center of the world". I told him that I was aware of all the things he was telling me. Then he said emphatically that he knew that his roots were in Africa. I agreed with him on that notion. He smiled and said, "I like Africans you know." I was glad. That was a window of opportunity for me to continue to work with him so that he would leave Marianne alone.

Suddenly, he released his strangle hold on Marianne who was now lying flat on the floor. I was afraid she was unconscious. I even wondered why one of the neighbours did not call the police; so that I won't have to do the police work! Jason ran to his mother and began to cry. I lifted her up from the floor and placed her on the sofa. He followed her to the sofa and continued crying. She opened her eyes that were closed, until then; she began to regain consciousness, then she looked at me as if that was a cue for her, she started to cry uncontrollably "Ain't nothing wrong with her man". Jahman said. I looked at Jahman and said "Please Jahman, just take it easy okay. Remember your son. She is the one who will take care of him." Jahman nodded, half-heartedly, brought out his marijuana, placed it in his mouth, but did not light it. He hugged his son for such a prolonged time, and to my surprise, I saw tears well up in his eyes. He was struggling not to cry; to be a man in front of his son. For a moment, I was happy that at least something cracked inside him to make him see reason. His son cried. He rubbed his long, brown, curly hair with his large hands as before. Jason hugged him, apparently glad he had stopped battering his mum, and told his dad that he loved him. Then, Jahman walked up to Marianne, knelt down by the sofa, and told her that he was sorry, but she did not say anything in response to his apology. Again, Jahman tried to cry, but he controlled himself. He brought out a big handkerchief which was red, gold, and green in colour, and dabbed his eyes with it. She was shaking as if she was incredibly cold. I believed that was because he had traumatized her. At that moment, the sight of him kneeling down and begging her repulsed Marianne. When he saw that she was not responding to his apology, he came to me, gave me a bear hug and said that he was sorry about what he did, that he knew he had made a fool of himself, and that he had disgraced himself in front of his son. Then he said: "I've been an asshole man". His nose twitched involuntarily. I fixed my gaze on the beginning of gray hair that protruded defiantly from his nostrils. Then, I told him that Marianne was really devastated and that he should never lay his hands on her again. He nodded absent-mindedly and suddenly he said: "Jah Rastafari!" showed a clenched fist in the Black Panther fashion, and waved goodbye to his son, who was still crying. Moments later, he left the apartment.

I had been familiar with one of the musicians in the group - *Light of Zion,* whose name was

John Koh. He was actually from Cameroun, but he was a reggae enthusiast and a friend to Jahman. John Koh had asked me to compose a reggae song for the group, but I told him that I couldn't. He kept pestering me, insisting that he heard that, apart from being a playwright, I was also a poet. Finally, I agreed to write the lyrics to this tune I called *Babylon Reggae.* I told my West African friend, John Koh, not to show it to the group, because I thought it was not good enough, but he showed it to them anyway, and joked that when they make their second album, they would include *Babylon Reggae* in it and that when the royalties come, I would get my share of it. This was the lyrics of *Babylon Reggae* that I composed for the group in 1978.

"Babylon reggae
It's for you and me
Babylon reggae
It's for natty dread locks
Oh! Natty dread, dread
Natty dread!   (Chorus)
Why you are in a Babylon?
Natty dread   (Chorus)
Oh! Natty dread, dread
Natty dread   (Chorus)
Why you are in a Shanty Town?
Natty Dread   (Chorus)
Oh! Natty dread lock
In a Babylon   (Chorus)
Oh! Natty dread lock
Is a Lion   (Chorus)
Oh! Natty, dread, dread
Waiting for Zion   (Chorus)
So Babylon reggae
It's for natty dread locks
Babylon
reggae
Is for you
and me.
Oh! Natty dread lock
Natty dread.   (Chorus)
Why you are in a Babylon?
Natty dread.   (Chorus)

(Lyrics of *Babylon Reggae*, Dipo Kalejaiye August 1978.)

The production of *The Father of Secrets* occurred in early January 1985. Marianne and her son came to see the play. I was shocked to see Jahman in the very back row, with his beard much longer, and with a hint of gray in it. He wore a red gold and green knit beret to cover part of his dreadlocks. Of course, red gold, and green were the official colours of the Rastafarians. The colours seemed to appear in almost everything Rastafarian. He was also dressed in a pseudo suit with a very clean white shirt and a tie to match, an expensive pair of pants, and a pair of shiny black shoes. Except for the wool knit Rastafarian beret, he looked like he might be a candidate for a job interview. He seemed to be a bit subdued. Marianne and her son did not notice him as he was the last person to enter when the theatre lights had been dimmed for the commencement of the play. Perhaps, after the incident in which he beat her up, he kept hanging around the city of Berkeley, where Marianne lived, and where the theatre was located. Obviously, his son was always on his mind, and he was trying not to be too far away from him. Marianne had forgiven him for the beatings she received from him, but had gone back to court to get a complete restraining order against Jahman. That meant that if Jahman wanted to see his son, he would have to see him in a public place, like a theatre, a restaurant, or even in the lobby of a movie house, with his mother there, and in full view of at least three persons. I guessed that was to discourage Jahman from being violent.

 Two persons of interest to me entered the theatre before Jahman. They were my former professor at the University of California at Berkeley, Professor Dunbar H. Ogden, and an African American movie star Art Evans.

Ogden had taught me medieval theatre history at Berkeley during my undergraduate years, a subject in which he was very knowledgeable. At that time, everyone wanted to be in his medieval theatre history class. He kindled my interest in that subject, although, I was always fascinated by history anyway. He would go on to become a master of that subject, writing numerous scholarly articles about it that would eventually culminate in definitive books on medieval theatre history. I had invited him to the production, but he had told me that his teaching, research, and writing engagements may make him unavailable to come and see it. In fact, the week of the production he was supposed to be in Sweden for a Scandinavian

Conference on Medieval Theatre History. At any rate, I was
surprised and happy to see Ogden. I knew that at the end of the
play, he would have something to say to me about the production. I
tiptoed to where he sat in the front row of the theatre and greeted
him, and we had a warm handshake.

Art Evans, on the other hand, had been invited by Mrs. Vaughn. He
was in San Francisco, giving a talk about his new movie at the time
known as *A Soldier's Story*. The movie had been nominated for
three Oscars. He had played the role of Private Wilkie in that
movie. Mrs. Vaughn wanted to use his appearance at the Black
Repertory Theatre's production of my play to showcase the fact that
African Americans can achieve whatever they want if they put their
minds to it. Art Evans came as an example of an African American
achiever. Later, after the show, he insisted that I should take a
picture with him. Interestingly, a young girl of about seven years
old at the time jumped in with us and insisted she wanted to be in
the picture too. She was the daughter of one of the volunteers of the
theatre. To this date, I still have that picture.

There were about forty people in the theatre that only sits about
fifty- five comfortably. I was eager to see how Sam Oni would
perform. He seemed pseudo-Yoruba to me, having been so imbibed
with Ghanaian culture of the Twi, and Ewe people. I saw the theatre
lights go off, and my heart began to pound. Questions began to
roam my mind such as: What if he forgot his lines, How about the
pronunciation of the Yoruba words in the play, How about the
synchronization of action and movement; the use of space, the
mastery of appropriate gestures and basic projection, which were
some of the characteristics of a good actor. The performance was
for an American audience and I was worried that the Yoruba
nuances of the play might be lost to that audience. The main
character spoke in incantations, and in a deeply rooted Yoruba
rhetorical manner complete with proverbs and philosophy. I thought
someone who was Yoruba but had spent so much of his life in
Ghana like Sam Oni, may be unable to cope with this issue. But as
the play progressed, I was impressed by Sam's verbiage and

tenacity. The play was only about an hour on stage. Everyone clapped when the performance ended. There was a question and answer session after the production. I tried to answer as many questions as I could, and I let the cast and crew handle some of the other questions. Professor Ogden wanted me to change the ending of the play, but that would have made the satire inherent in the action of the lead character more like a regular comedy or slapstick. I told him I did not think that it was a good idea to change the ending as he had suggested because that would kill the meaning of the play.

 Art Evans congratulated me on the success of the production and asked when I was going to have another of my play staged at the Black Repertory. I became curious about him. Part of my aim in returning to the United States was getting a possible connection into entering Hollywood as an actor. I knew that one needed a kind of good connection in order to achieve a feat of that nature. There were not too many African actors in Hollywood. I had met the late Pa Orlando Martins in Calabar in 1983. He was a Nigerian movie actor who co-starred with Ronald Reagan in a Hollywood film - *Sanders of the River (1935)*. He offered a rendition of Paul Robeson's singing of a song in the movie – '*Ol Man River.*' Pa Orlando's sang the song this way:

Johhny rows the boat, down the
river, Yegede o!
Johnny rows the boat down the
river Yegede oooo!
Ahaha! Ahaha! Ahaha!
Johnny rows the boat down the
river Yegede ooo!

I was impressed by his booming and vibrating voice I still remember carrying his coat at the time and listening to him complain that it was terrible for a man in his eighties to be fighting cataracts! He had been invited by the University of Calabar to come and give a talk on movie acting. He was an ebullient fellow. That meeting was my closest to Hollywood at that time. Art Evans seemed like a very decent human being, and he joked and laughed a lot. In essence, he was a jolly man who was graying at the time, and I thought either his gray appeared too soon, or it was hereditary. I wanted to ask him how one could "break into Hollywood" so to speak, but too many people bombarded him with questions, asked for his autograph, and played around as if they had been his friends for such a long time. I began to see the trials of being a celebrity. He gave me an autographed black and white picture of him from the movie- *A Soldier's Story*. Interestingly, he was a Berkeley native, having been born in Berkeley and gone to school there. I wanted to get his phone number after the show that night, but Mary Dobson, Sam's girlfriend kept talking to him and it looked as if she was going to talk his ears off. I saw him scribble something on a paper that he gave to Mary Dobson, and my heart sank. I thought Mary was going to monopolize him so that no one would be able to get close to Art Evans. I could see a few people lounging around in the theatre, and in the middle of them where Marianne, Jahman, and Jason. The people represented the court ordered mandatory ones who must be around in a public place in order for Jahman to see his son.

Soon after the production of *The Father of Secrets*, I left Marianne's house, not knowing where I was going to go and live. Of course, I was still not financially buoyant, and the issue of paying for rent did not cross my mind at all. Marianne was full of gratitude for the way I handled Jahman and his violent nature and pleaded with me not to leave. She said Jason was getting used to me and that he would be devastated by my departure. I was not convinced by that because I was sure Jason knew who his father was, and his emotional attachment would have been to his father and not to me. I knew I had to get a place first, before looking for a job. While Marianne was trying to persuade me not to leave, Jason heard our discussion and said: "Mum is Dipo leaving?" Marianne told him I was not, but the boy seemed to know better as he grinned in utmost satisfaction as if contented that it was good I was leaving. To him, I had become someone who was competing with him for his mother's affection. There would be no one to prevent him from watching re-runs of *Dracula* or *Frankenstein,* television movies that Marianne insisted I should not let him watch.

Incidentally, a member of the audience on that night of the production of *The Father of Secrets* was Luisah Teish. I had known her when I was an undergraduate at Berkeley, but had lost contact with her after I graduated from the university. I was not sure how she found out about the play, but she came to see the play with her sister. We greeted each other warmly, and I seized the opportunity to tell her that I was looking for an apartment to rent, as my wife and children would soon arrive from Nigeria and we could not all be living in Marianne's apartment! She told me that there was a basement apartment vacant in her big house in North Oakland and that if I would like, I should come and see it the next day. I did not know how I was going to get the money to pay for the apartment, but I knew that if she gave me the apartment, I would quickly get any menial job that was available and promise to pay her at the end of January The next day, I quickly got out to go to the house in North Oakland and to inspect the apartment. It seemed manageable for a family of five. I was sure that barring any immigration problems, my wife and children should join me in the United States in 1985. A few days after I inspected the basement apartment in the Luisah Teish's house, I moved into it.

It was still 1985 when The Black repertory contacted me saying that they were interested in my new play *The Graduate Palava.* Apparently, the movie actor had mentioned to Mrs Vaughn that it would be nice to have another one of my plays staged at the theatre. Mrs. Vaughn asked if I had another play that could be staged at the theatre. I told her that I had just finished writing *The Graduate Palava* before I left the University of Calabar and that the play was even under contract with Macmillan Publishers London, for publication. She seemed excited when I told her this, then she asked me how many characters were in the play. I told her that there were only four characters in the play. It was then that she told me that there was a condition, and it was that I had to direct the play myself because they could not find a director for it. She said the directors of the theatre were a bit hesitant about directing an African play and that they had complained that they would not be able to handle the African nuances of the play. I thought I could get a small stipend for directing the play, but Mrs Vaughn told me that the theatre was a community theatre and that there was no chance that I could be paid for my directorial services. I began to think of going to the Employment Office and looking for any menial job I could find. I knew that with the impending arrival of my family, the pressure would be great for me to support the family. There was no chance that I would be able to get them to sleep on "table-beds" or endure the cold without heat or food. Perhaps I could not ask them to live the type of bohemian life I lived when I first arrived in the United States. I accepted Mrs. Vaughn's offer and began a two-pronged attempt of looking for a job and looking for actors for *The Graduate Palava.*

Luisah had been generous enough to let me move into the apartment without paying until the end of the month. I told her that by then I would have worked for one month and would have been able to pay the rent. I bought *The Oakland Tribune* and *The San Francisco Chronicle* whenever I could afford to do so, and perused the papers looking first in the Employment Section, to see if I could find any menial job that would fit me. Whenever I could not afford to buy the papers, I would go to the train station and pick up any one someone might have inadvertently left on the benches of the train station. I used to apply to as many as fifteen or twenty menial jobs a day. I was serious then, about getting any kind of job I could find. However, I did not think of the logistics that was involved in trying to get to fifteen or twenty places in a day! I would call the manager of an establishment and make an appointment. Sometimes, the appointment would be for an interview or just so the manager of the establishment could meet me. If I made an appointment with a manager that I could not keep, I would quickly call the manager to shift it to the next day. I did this with almost all the establishments I tried to apply to. The whole thing was an ordeal indeed. I got to a restaurant where I was seeking a job, and everyone that worked there was white. The Owner took one look at me and said that the position was filled! She continued to smoke her cigarettes and to talk to a man she kept calling Henry and ignored me where I stood pleading for the position!

I could see some of the waitresses in their red and white skirts and blouses in the dining area of the restaurant. They stopped what they were doing, and congregated in clusters laughing and pointing at me. Obviously, they were thinking that I had made a mistake coming to apply to work in that restaurant. I was incensed, but there was nothing I could do. I had no proof that the owner of the restaurant had discriminated against me because I was black. Someone told me that the Chinese Restaurant in the Chinatown area of Oakland was hiring, so I went there. My experience was different from the other one in which I felt discriminated against. When I got there, everyone looked at me with a certain curiosity. They all spoke Chinese. They just kept looking at me and speaking in Chinese! (It was later, that I was told that they were actually speaking Mandarin) I stood there for a while, and then a beautiful Chinese lady, apparently, a waitress, and part owner of the restaurant tried to walk me to one of the eating booths, mistaking me for a customer! I tried to tell her that I was not there to eat, but she kept smiling and pointing at the booth, and asking me to sit down. She then walked up to me and stroked my arm, smiling and still asking me to sit down. Angry and frustrated, I bolted out of the restaurant even as the lady held out her outstretched hands as if asking me to come back, and that the food will be delicious! Finally, I applied for the position of a dishwasher at a restaurant known as *India-Kashmir Restaurant* in Albany. The town was near Berkeley. The day I went for the interview, I was surprised to note how friendly Mr. Shivaji, the owner was. He asked me interesting questions about Nigeria, and that he had relatives in Lagos. He commented about Indian food being a bit like Nigerian food since we both use spices and seasonings in our meals. He even told me that one day he would visit Nigeria. As Mr. Shivaji was being generally pleasant and civil with me, his wife appeared. She was a co-owner of the restaurant. She too was very nice to me when she saw how Mr. Shivaji was joking and laughing with me even in an interview. The interview turned out to be a pleasant conversation between two friends, which ended up in-jokes and laughter. "You must start *vork* tomorrow." Mr. Shivaji said in his thick Indian accent, pronouncing the word 'work' as '*vork*'. "I *vill* pay you three dollars and fifty cents per hour." He said as he got up, shook hands with me and excused himself. I agreed to the offer knowing fully well that dishwashers did not get paid that much at all. The owners were very generous with me, allowing me to take home left over foods like madras – tender meat cooked with coconut and fresh spices, tandori lamb chops, and curried chicken. I was, eating well, and was even throwing food away! Also, I began to save a little out of my weekly pay as a dishwasher. But the weekly pay was grossly inadequate and it was nearing the arrival of my family. In essence, "the heat was on".

The dishwashing work was tedious. A lot of times the dishwashing machine would break down and I would have to wash the dishes by hand. I would complain to Mr. Shivaji, but he would either ignore my complaints or say that the technician was coming to fix the archaic machines. It would seem like ages and I would see no technician. Finally, when he arrived, he would do a haphazard job on the two machines, and they would break down again. In that case, I had to soak the dishes in hot water in the double sink in the kitchen. I would wash in one sink, and rinse in the other. The hot water would be so hot; it would make my hands white and flaky. Then, I devised a method of using huge rubber gloves on both hands. The gloves would reach my elbow, yet, the heat would penetrate them into my hands, and when I removed the gloves; my hands would look baked! The restaurant was popular with the elites of Albany and Berkeley, who wanted an exotic dinner outing.

Wednesdays through Sundays were very busy days. The dishes would pile up incredibly, and I used to look at them, even as I throw some curried lamb and rice into my mouth, wondering if I would ever be able to finish washing the dishes for that day. I was usually envious of the waiters and the waitresses as they were always able to finish their work on time and leave. I would be the very last person to leave the restaurant, as I could not leave unless there were no customers eating in the restaurant, and no dishes to be washed. On occasions, I would notice a few doting couples looking at themselves through the romantic orange and blue neon lights of the restaurant and they would be eating so slowly. Sometimes, they would stop to kiss each other, before they would continue to eat again. I was usually exasperated about that. The reason for that was simple; I was going to be in the restaurant a long time that night. Actually, that was good in the sense that I made more money through overtime pay. The owners of the restaurant could not ask them to leave while they were still consuming their meals. The closing time for the restaurant was about 10:30 p.m., but customers could remain in the restaurant till about midnight.

It was about February of 1985, and I had been working in *India-Kashmir Restaurant* for about a month, when Mr. Shivaji, the owner of the restaurant, called me and told me that he wanted to talk to me. I sat down in front of him and he even asked me to go and get a cup of coffee if I wanted. I suspected his motivation in that it felt as if he was trying to make me feel relaxed for what he wanted to say. I fixed my gaze on his Pagari - Indian turban, his trademark silver bracelet – the Kara, and his heavy mustache and beard. Mr. Shivaji, a Sikh, was always dressed in this typical Sikh fashion. His brownish-gray eyes sparkled in the late afternoon sun. I heard the screeching of two of the Bart trains coming to a halt at the Albany Station, not too far from the restaurant. Then I heard the heavy dragging of their alloyed wheels on the rail tracks as the train moved again to the next station. "Dipo, I am sorry to say that I *vill* no longer need your services. Business is slow and I can't afford to keep you" he said in a nonchalant attitude as he lighted a cigarette.

He blew the smoke away from us and coughed as if he was just learning to smoke. I watched him straighten up his tie and he placed his elbows on the table looking intently into my eyes. His wife was busy working behind the counter, cleaning wine glasses with a certain practiced perfection, and placing them in their little holes in wooden swivel racks behind the counter. Occasionally, she would look up as if she was trying to look at me without my knowing it. Mrs. Shivaji really liked me and I could tell by her look that she was trying to exonerate herself from her husband's decision to sack me. It was as if she was saying: "Look, it's his decision to let you go, I have no hand in it."

There was silence between us, as he drew a few puffs of the cigarette, and coughed as before. I wanted to tell him not to smoke if he did not know how to do it without getting the smoke into his lungs and coughing. As if he was reading my thoughts, he put out the cigarette on the silver ashtray on the table, and picked up his cup of tea, sipping it as if it was exotic. He drank a lot of tea. "But where do you want me to go Mr. Shivaji, I need this job, and my family is arriving from Nigeria in a few months". When I finished speaking, he looked at me and smiled, taking the time to speak in a measured tone." I am *wery*, *wery,* sorry, but business is *wery* slow and we have to close the restaurant for about four days a week, we *vill* only open it only on Friday, Saturday, and Sunday." I was disappointed. Obviously, Mr. Shivaji's decision was a business decision for which he cannot be faulted. I accepted my fate. "I *vill* give you your pay for this *veek* that you have *vorked*, and you *vill* not need to come back tomorrow." He said as he got up to try and join his wife who was still busy cleaning the wine glasses and placing them on the swivel rack, all the time avoiding my eyes. That was how I lost the dishwashing job at *India Kashmir Restaurant*. After losing this job, I decided I must find any other job to replace it. I had now graduated into looking for menial jobs, as no one was hiring College Instructors – the type of job Dr. Sam Oni had. The month was racing to an end. I would have to pay Luisah Teish at the end of February.

My wife had told me that they were likely to arrive in the U.S.A sometime in May or June of 1985. That was only a few months from February. I had to act quickly and decisively. I had not abandoned the challenge that the Black Repertory Theatre imposed upon me to direct my play – *The Graduate Palava*. I was still looking for actors for the play. Then one day I heard that the Nigerian musician Johhny Haastrup who was living in the San Francisco Bay Area at the time was going to play at *Ashkenaz*. I resolved to go there and try to find him and to ask if he would be interested in playing the role of Ilori, the unemployed graduate in the play. Unfortunately, I was unable to go to *Ashkenaz* to look for him on the day of his gig at the nightclub. However, someone directed Johhny Haastrup to the Black Repertory Theatre. The person told him that a Nigerian play was going to be staged in the theatre. I think that brought him to the theatre. It was a rarity indeed for a Nigerian, or African play to be staged in the area at that time. He arrived at the theatre with my friend Babatunde Kayode, one day when I was in the theatre discussing the preparation for the play with Mrs. Vaughn. I was happy to see them and I asked them to wait in the lobby. When I finished my conversation with Mrs Vaughn, I walked up to Johnny Haastrup and we hugged. He had been the leader of a band in Nigeria known as *Monomono* (Lightning). I told him that I wanted him to play the role of Ilori Adakodana, the unemployed graduate in the play. I had never met Johnny before then, but when I was in Nigeria, and just fresh out of the secondary school, I joined a group known as *The Benders*, and his brother, Segun Haastrup was the lead guitarist for the group. The leader of the group was the iconic Soyinka actor – Tunji Oyelana. At the time, it seemed as if Johnny was looking for new challenges other than music, and the opportunity that the impending stage production presented seemed to be the alternative he was looking for.

It was now the middle of March 1985. I had gotten a phone call from my wife that the American Embassy in Lagos had given them the visa they had been waiting for. She was so elated. They were likely to arrive in the U.S.A in May of that year. She seemed quite excited while talking to me on the phone, but I only pretended that I was happy about the development. I did not have a steady job, and that made me rather calm during my conversation with her. Incidentally, I got another dishwashing job at a Berkeley Marina Restaurant. The job was pretty much the same drab one like the one in *India- Kashmir Restaurant*. The work was tedious, and of course, the dishwashing machine broke down several times! The only thing I could think about concerning the machines was that they stopped working because of heavy use. More times than not, I was again, washing dishes by hand, in hot water, with my hands caking up and whitish as before.

The owner was Mrs. Clara Herrick, a woman of Scandinavian roots, but whom everyone called "Clara", or "Miss Clara". She was a rather sophisticated woman who smoked her cigarettes with a cigarette holder. Her favourite drink was a drink known as – 'Bloody Mary', which she would order the barman to prepare for her every four 0'clock in the evening. When she could not get the Bloody Mary, she would settle for gin and lime. This was the only restaurant where I worked, where two of the waitresses thought I was "cute"! The day one of them said that to me, I pulled out my wedding ring from my pocket and showed it to her, and I told her that I was married and that my wife had just arrived from Nigeria. She giggled and said that if my wife had truly arrived from Nigeria, how come she had never come to the restaurant to see me? I did not bother to reply to her question. I was in the habit of putting the ring in my pocket so that it would not be damaged by the hot water I constantly placed my hands in as I washed the dishes. Apart from that, one day, I had chipped off the edges of one of the plates with the robust ring. I heard one of the rather busy body waitresses say "Dipo broke a plate … It became a sing-song among the waitresses "Dipo broke a plate …" Almost like an abandoned nursery rhyme potent enough to bore a child in a nursery school. "Dipo broke a plate... Dipo broke a plate." When they stopped singing their annoying nursery rhyme, one of them said: "Oh! Oh! Oh! Miss

Clara is going to make you pay for it". In that restaurant at the time, it was taboo for a dishwasher to break a plate. Apparently, too many dishes had broken and Clara had instituted a policy. It was that the offending dishwasher would have to pay for the broken plate from his wages. Clara said she was tired of replacing broken plates every week. There was a rumour that one Hispanic dishwasher who worked there before me – Jose Hernandez, was really very clumsy and lazy and that when he did not want to wash the dishes, by hand, of course, he would break them and throw them into the trash can! I guessed Clara wanted to make sure that no one broke her plates deliberately, hence the policy she instituted. Amazingly, I think I was the only black man that worked in the restaurant, and I heard that Clara, was a kind of a world traveller, and that gave her a wider view of the world. This, according to Joseph, the barman was why she did not discriminate against anyone who wanted to work in her restaurant.

But I think Mrs. Herrick was involved in insurance fraud; she had set her restaurant on fire just so that she could collect insurance money! Although, I knew at the time that the restaurant was not making money, yet, Clara refused to let any of her employees go! To me, I thought she had a little of the bohemian lifestyle in her. I got there an hour after the suspicious fire gutted the restaurant and no one needed to tell me that there was no work for me or anyone else employed by Clara. She was standing outside the burnt restaurant when the firefighters, police, and the emergency medical team arrived. I looked at the charred remains of the well-built restaurant and I was shocked. Burnt chairs, tables, and roof top that had caved in to allow the bright sun rays into what was left of the restaurant, it was a pity to behold. A few of the waitresses were standing by the fire hoses and shaking like people caught in the frozen cold of a winter storm. The staccato voices of radio talk back and forth with the police, and firemen punctuated the air. I heard something like this:

Yes, come in Tom… No, it's the Berkeley Marina Restaurant. Yes. On University Avenue. No, Ms. Clara Herrick… Yes, that's the owner. No one injured over. No. Just third-degree burns… completely treatable. No deaths. Over… You better send another ambulance. Yes, we may have to cordon off the area. Yes. There is a yellow tape around the remains of the restaurant. Yes, I understand, no one in or out of it Roger. Yes, thanks over and out, Roger.

 She looked at me calmly and said nothing, smoking her cigarette out of a long cigarette holder. She wore a blue dress which made her look regal to me, and I could not understand the fact that she could have deliberately set the fire. The restaurant was never rebuilt, and no one knew what became of the woman and the insurance money she got. Much later on, I heard that she had moved to Reno, Nevada, and had opened another restaurant for the gambling clientele of "the biggest little city in the world."
 A friend of mine, who was a cab driver, told me that there was a lot of money in that venture. He said that even in New York, there were many people with PhDs who were driving cabs and that cab-driving was actually a profitable profession. He said even many Nigerians who had PhDs and could not get jobs were driving cabs. My friend even said that when some of these Nigerian cab drivers get back to Nigeria on vacation and they were spending their dollars, no one would ask them whether they made the money from cab driving or from another job. I had been thinking of what I could be doing to sustain my family and myself, while I was waiting to be employed at a community college as an Instructor. That had always been my wish. Sam Oni was employed at Laney College, and I had also been interested in that kind of position, but because the college Instructor positions were always so competitive, it seemed rather difficult to get one. My friend, Segun, kept calling me and advising me to try working as a cab driver. He told me that at least, I would take money home every day. After so much cajoling from him, I resolved to apply to the Goodwill Cab Company in Oakland California.

The production of *The Graduate Palava* was slated for April 1985. Apart from working in a restaurant, I tried to fix rehearsals in the evenings that I was off from work. Trying to fix a time that would be convenient for the four actors was a real challenge as everyone's schedule was quite different. Finally, we agreed on Tuesday and Thursday evenings, and Sunday at noon. I was lucky to get Johnny Haastrup, as the unemployed graduate, and Daisy Moore, an African American woman, as his equally unemployed girlfriend. Unfortunately, Daisy Moore had to drop out of the play, and I replaced her with a very serious African American actress- Elana Dorsey. A wise cracking Nigerian man, who was also a cab driver, Sola Adediran, agreed to play the role of the indefatigable Managing Director. Babatunde Kayode agreed to play the role of the weird psychiatrist, who was a friend to the unemployed graduate – Ilori Adakodana. Babatunde, with his very bushy beard and flamboyant character, was a sight to behold on stage! Even in rehearsals, he was serious, hardly took a break, even if I called for one. During the break that I had called, he would eat his fish sandwich, which he bought from the store of the Black Muslims that was around the corner from the theatre. He hated meat; he only ate fish, but smoked marijuana abundantly. He was the one who would remind me that the thirty- minute break was over and we should get back to work. He was an artist to the core, one who dabbled in music, film, arts, painting, and acting. He seemed always thrilled whenever he was with me, offering advice on the different artistic projects we could be involved in. It got to a point that I counted about seven projects and I could not make up my mind, which one we should zero on first. It was Babatunde who often tried to keep Sola Adediran in check when the latter would be involved in his many horse-playing sessions, which often disrupted the rehearsals. When of course he was weaned out of the horseplay, he would begin jokes that made everybody laugh. The laughter, then made them forget their lines and blockings and I would have to start all over again, redoing the stage blockings and insisting that their dialogue and movement must match. He exhibited verbal theatrics that was uncanny, and he was always complaining that he was hungry, even after eating voraciously in front of everyone just before the beginning of the rehearsal!

One day, to make matters worse, he asked me to produce his girlfriend before he could participate in the rehearsals! He said he was lonely for her. I told him that I was sorry, but he had so many girlfriends, perhaps one for every day, and that I was not sure which one he wanted me to produce. Everyone laughed and the rehearsals began in earnest. Elana Dorsey, the stunningly beautiful actress that played Kike was always amused about the behaviour of Sola Adediran, but she was the tempering voice in the cast, and everyone listened to her when she would say "it's enough, let us continue with the rehearsals" Sola would stop all his clowning, and surprisingly, he would know all his lines. Sola even told Elana that he wanted her to be his girlfriend and that he would take her to Ibadan, his hometown in Nigeria, and make her eat the local meal of *amala* and *ewedu*. Elana merely laughed and hugged him and said that she wanted to be his girlfriend too! Everyone laughed at Sola's silliness and appreciated her warmth and camaraderie. She was a lady of great decorum and class, and very serious about the business of acting. If we needed something for the rehearsal, and we could not get it, she would go out of her way to produce it; anything to make sure the production was successful was her forte. Even on the eve of the actual opening, I asked Babatunde whether Sola would be able to handle his lines properly and to play the part convincingly. He told me not to worry and that everything would be okay. I was annoyed because I thought he was holding brief for Sola who might mess up the performance.

Since the production was still part of the Black Repertory Theatre's New Arts Experience Program, performances were on Sunday evenings only, for a month. The advertisement for the play appeared in *The Berkeley Express* this way:

Black Repertory Theatre's New Arts Experience Program presents The Graduate Palava - A play written by a Nigerian – Dipo

Kalejaiye. It is a Nigerian social satire treating the issue of graduate unemployment... The play runs on Sundays only through the month of April. Show time is 8:30.p.m at 1719 Alcatraz Avenue Berkeley. 652-2120.

A theatre critic Jim Herron sneaked into the theatre one night during the performance. I did not see him when he came in, but when the performance was over, he asked me to grant him an interview. I obliged him, and we sat in front of the stage after the show was over. He asked me a few questions about the play and Nigeria. It was on the 18th of April 1985 that a review by Jim Herron came out in *The Berkeley Express*. Part of the review reads this way:

"The tragicomic play follows the travails of college graduate –Ilori Adakodana a frustrated job seeker in modern day Nigeria. It succeeds in keeping the audience laughing with both silliness and pointed sarcasm. Some members of the audience did not understand one scene in which the fiancé seemed to go into a trance. It was explained that she was possessed by an 'Abiku' the spirit of a deceased infant that manifested itself in the form of seizures and fainting spells. The interplay between characters picked up momentum as the play went along. The most sardonic moments came when Babatunde Kayode (the Psychiatrist) was reading aloud the entries he was writing about Adakodana's case. Sola Adediran was very good as the unctuous Managing Director. Johnny Haastrup turned in a credible performance in a difficult role as Adakodana, the somewhat serious though more often ridiculous job seeker" (*The Berkeley Review* 18th April 1985).

I had been pestering Mrs, Vaughn to write a letter of recommendation for me for the position of an Instructor, which opened up at Laney College in Oakland. The college was part of a consortium of three colleges under the auspices of The Peralta

Community College District. Initially, her busy schedule did not allow her to write the letter of recommendation, but finally, she instructed her secretary to write the letter. I was so excited the day the secretary told me that she had been instructed to write the letter. Mrs. Vaughn was very careful in appending her signature to anything, be it a letter, or any other document. I sat in the office of the secretary in the morning that she typed the letter. She had been instructed to give me the letter to read, and if I was satisfied with the recommendation, Mrs. Vaughn would sign it. This was the letter.

Ms. Patty Savage
Personnel Office
Peralta Community College District
333East 8th Street
Oakland, CA.
94607.

April 4, 1985.

Ms. Savage:

I have been acquainted with Oladipo (Dipo) Kalejaiye for over five years. My initial introduction to him was as a result of his participation in the Black Repertory Theatre's New Arts Experience Program; a program designed to showcase the works of new playwrights.

I found him to be a very interesting and talented person with a deep commitment to his work; as evidenced through the mounting of several of his one-act plays (one of which he directed.)

Mr. Kalejaiye is an outstanding young man whose attributes would be an asset to any program or project.

Nora. B. Vaughn
Executive Director.

Mrs. Vaughn sent this recommendation to The Peralta Community College District, but the copy reproduced above was only my own copy of the letter. I was excited. At least I would be back in the academic environment, possibly, teaching at Laney College. Teaching had always been my passion. I went to the drama department of the college one day. I had invited myself on a tour of that department. When I entered the Department of Drama, everyone looked at me curiously. They instinctively knew that I was a stranger and had not been invited, the way I was looking around and trying to find someone to talk to. The Chairperson of the department was Mr. Lew Levinson, who seemed to be excited that I had applied and that he was looking forward to my joining the drama department. He seemed like a very nice man and his wife was a student in the department as well. Still, I was not too sure that I would be called for an interview. I was looking for more people to write on my behalf.

Luckily for me, Adam David Miller, an African American poet, who taught in the English Department of Laney, agreed to write another letter of recommendation on my behalf. He was well known in the San Francisco Bay Area, as a poet.

He had seen at least three of my plays staged at The Black Repertory Theatre, one of them was *The Creator and the Disrupter* in which Jimi Solanke, the talented Soyinka actor, played the lead role of Obatala, the god of creation.

My plan was simple: I knew that Adam taught at Laney College, and that could help to bolster my chances of getting hired by the college. I remember going to his house, somewhere in Berkeley, not too far from the theatre, essentially to talk about my aspiration for teaching. I also attended the poetry workshops he organized in his home. During those workshops, he was usually generous, making sure that cakes, pies, tea, and coffee, were available for everyone before they dispersed at about 9.p.m He seemed sympathetic, but kept promising to write a letter of reference for me which to me at the time, he took forever to write. In fairness to him, he was a very busy man. He was, among other things, a Teacher, Poet, Critic, Radio Commentator, and Community Activist. He was soft spoken and intelligent, and I was happy to be associated with him because of his wisdom and quiet charisma. I heard that he had been associated with many writers, African American writers like Nikki Giovanni, Ishmael Reed, Ed Bullins, Alice Walker, and Toni Morrison. Finally, after much pestering from me he wrote this reference letter on my behalf:

April 30, 1985
"This is to recommend Oladipo Kalejaiye for a position in theatre at Laney College. I have known Mr. Kalejaiye for more than three years, both during his years at San Jose State University, and his work with the Black Repertory Theatre Group in Berkeley. I have admired his work in theatre, both as a writer and as a director. His experience as a teacher and director in his home country, Nigeria, has added to this admiration. I have found him diligent and conscientious in his work and helpful in his dealings with others. He made a fine contribution to the workshops he attended. With his training, experience, and attitude, I feel that Mr. Kalejaiye would, make a welcome addition to the Laney Theatre Department."
Adam David Miller
Department of English
Laney College
.

After Adam wrote this recommendation on my behalf, I began to walk around Laney as if I had been given the position. I went back to the Theatre department to talk to Mr. Lew Levinson, who said he was glad to see me again. I wanted to know if Adam's note to the college had precipitated the desired effect. He did not mention the letter, or whether I had been called for an interview. Really, I was not expecting him to mention such a thing to me as it was an administrative matter, and he was not a member of the Personnel

Department of the college. Lew only took me on another tour of the theatre department and I left the Laney college campus. The college did not hire me for the full-time regular position I was seeking but gave me a substitute position as an Instructor in the Theatre Department. Of course, I could only come in as a substitute if one of the Instructors did not come to teach. At that time, it seemed that everyone decided to show up for their jobs in the theatre department, even if they were ill! I felt disappointed as I had to begin work as a cab driver. I had been given the position, but did not actually start working hoping that I would get the Laney College job. The dispatcher at the Cab Company had also called me to ask if I was no longer interested in cab driving.

Chapter: 3 (At Ile Orunmila/Oshun)

Jumoke and our
> three children arrived in the United States in May of 1985. I
> was then living in the rented two- bedroom apartment in the
> basement of Luisah Teish's and David Wilson's house.

In 1985, my wife, Jumoke, and I decided to start The Amuyo
African Theatre. Incidentally, my wife had studied Dramatic Arts at
the then University of Ife, under the tutelage of Wole Soyinka, who
was the head of the department while she was there. She advised
me that we could turn Yoruba folk tales into dramatic pieces,
complete with songs and dances. I thought the idea was brilliant as
we could actually charge for our performances. We decided that the
performances would be no more than an hour, or at most, an hour
and fifteen minutes, and the pieces would be referred to as *Folktale
Theatre*. We would perform at various locations such as *The La
Pena Cultural Centre* in Berkeley, and *The Western Addition* in San
Francisco. I began to look for members of the newly formed
Amuyo African Theatre Group. In fact, I wrote the following
proposal to Mrs. Vaughn, asking that the newly formed Theatre
Group be integrated into the Black Repertory Theatre. This was part
of the proposal:

May 25, 1985.
Dear Mrs. Vaughn,
Re: THE AMUYO AFRICAN THEATRE.
*I am sending you this proposal for your consideration because I
feel that the time is ripe enough for it. My association with the
Black Repertory Theatre began in 1976 when I was an
undergraduate at The University of California at Berkeley. My first
play, The Father of Secrets was produced at the theatre. Since then,
other plays such as Polygamy, Sure banker, The Creator and the
Disrupter, and The Chairman of the Board have been produced at
the theatre as well. After an association with the Black Repertory
Theatre, which is about nine years, I feel that it is time to solidify*

our union through cooperation between your theatre and my newly formed Amuyo African Theatre.

My wife Jumoke and I formed The Amuyo African Theatre because of our deep commitment to exposing African plays to the African American community. It is a project designed to capture the essence of African playwriting and theatre production, in order to transmit them in their proper perspectives to an audience for an appreciation of their African nuances, complexity, peculiar staging techniques, and entertainment value.

Amuyo African Theatre Company, with the support of The Black Repertory Theatre, will produce only plays by African playwrights of certain credibility and fame such as Wole Soyinka (Nigeria), Sarif Easmon (Sierra Leone), and Ama Ata Aidoo (Ghana). We will place emphasis on the more traditional and cultural African plays, as these will serve as a much-needed education on African culture and tradition for the community. There is very little in the area of authentic African Theatre in the San Francisco Bay Area, and this project could help to fill part of this large vacuum.

I propose that the Amuyo African Theatre Company becomes a fully integrated part of The Black Repertory Theatre, and also the main proponent of its African Theatre Program. At the moment, I am the Artistic Director of the company. It is also my plan to utilize some of the actors of The Black Repertory theatre in our African play production project.

My earlier intention to stage my newly published play – Polygyny (by Macmillan Publishers, London), has been suspended pending the outcome of The Black Repertory Theatre's reply to this proposal.

Yours Sincerely,
DIPO KALEJAIYE

In my proposal to the theatre, I did not mention the fact that *the Amuyo African Theatre* was going to be involved in performances outside of the *Black Repertory Theatre* as I was going to charge for those performances and I did not feel that any arrangement that included payment for the group would meet with a favourable response from Mrs. Vaughn. She did not seem to be too excited about my proposal when we discussed it. The issue of money arose and she told me that the theatre was operating on a shoestring budget, and it would be financially impossible to accommodate the extra performances that *The Amuyo African Theatre* was trying to bring into the theatre.

Meanwhile, Babatunde Kayode, my friend, who had played the role of the psychiatrist in my play *The Graduate Palava,* had been pestering me about jump-starting *The Amuyo African Theatre* which my wife and I had formed for the performance of Yoruba folktales. He argued that there was no use in starting a business and not following through with it. Finally, he convinced me to register the company in Alameda County and to make sure that the "Fictitious Business Name Statement" appeared in the *Oakland Tribune*. He said that would shield me from the charge of running an unlicensed business. He also said that I could then list my company as an item in my Income Tax returns. I took his advice and licensed the company in 1985. The notice appeared this way:

<u>Affidavit of Publication:</u>
In the matter of Amuyo African
Theatre P.O. Box 29556,
Oakland, California.
Affidavit of Publication Fictitious Business Name Statement
The State of California
County of Alameda   P. Maggy
Fictitious Business Name Statement.
The following persons are doing business as Amuyo African
Theatre, P. O. Box 29556,
Oakland, California, 94604, 1942 35th Avenue
Oakland, CA. 94604
1. Jumoke A. Kalejaiye
2. Dipo Kalejaiye.

The business is conducted by individuals –
husband and wife. Official seal: Leonard G. San
Juan Notary Public – California.
Alameda County 29th September 1985.

David was Luisah's flamboyant husband, who smoked a pipe all the time. Their relationship seemed interesting in a way. It was an association between a black woman and a white man. I was not really sure if they were actually married in the conventional sense of it, but at least they presented a united front as partners in their venture. David was a tall, blonde, and humorous man. He smoked a pipe to stimulate his salivary gland because, according to his doctor, his salivary glands did not secrete enough saliva. When he told me that, I did not know what to think, but I accepted his explanation. When I first started living in their house, David was still involved in what I may call "conventional employment." He was working as a detective, and one day, he startled me when he pulled out his gun and showed it to me. He was kind, generous, and understanding. It was later on, that he stopped working as a detective, and he faced the profession of being an Ifa Priest, - a Yoruba Babalawo. He reminded me of Susan Wenger, the Austrian woman who left her native Austria to come to Oshogbo in Nigeria, to live with the Yoruba people as an Orisha worshipper. I was amused in a way in that I asked him why he, a white man, was interested in the Ifa Oracle, but he only smiled and said that he was keenly interested in Ifa.

Luisah Teish, on the other hand, was a charismatic woman of formidable character, intelligence, and unabashed kindness. She was not as tall as her companion who stood well over six feet. She seemed to be a deeply southern woman with, of course, the famous 'southern hospitality' that we hear about all the time. As someone who had lived in Greensboro, North Carolina, in the southern part of the United States, I could recognize this bit of southern behaviour in her. Apart from this, there was something deeply enchanting, mystical and mysterious about her. She walked around as if she possessed a certain innate mystical knowledge about the universe in a distinctly New Orleans fashion. The Creole in her seemed to go back to its African roots. It was a mixture of wisdom, folklore, religion, magic, spirituality, feminism, and the harnessing of nature for personal benefit and improvement. She carried herself with a certain gait and confidence, always looking invincible even in the face of adversity.

I was perturbed about how to take care of the family whom I had not seen for about a year. Jumoke was a bit surprised about where I lived. She thought it had a certain mystery about it. She nosed around a little bit and concluded that something was odd about the activities that were going on at Ile Orunmila Oshun. Although aware of the Yoruba traditional religion, she was not a practitioner, and she felt that she should not be in an environment where it was practiced. Apart from that, she was concerned; the basement apartment was a little too small for a family of five. She advised me to look for a teaching position in one of the community colleges in the area. The children were growing and so were their needs. Luckily for me, I read in the *San Francisco Chronicle* that City College of San Francisco was hiring for Instructors in their drama department. I applied for the position, and was actually called for an interview because of, according to the letter inviting me for the interview, "your academic qualifications, talent, and creativity". At the interview, I was surprised to see only three candidates for the position waiting to be interviewed. Apart from my portfolio, Macmillan Publishers, London had just published my two plays – *Polygyny and Polyandry: Two Plays about Marriage*. I took a copy of the plays along to the interview. I thought I had a chance. It was a week after the interview that I found out that I did not get the position.

The job at the cab company looked more and more attractive to me. I did not want to let my family down. I knew what my friend was saying about taking money home every day. The job of a cab driver provided such an opportunity. After paying the cab company, one should have money left over that one could keep. The negative part of this was that if I made only seventy dollars, and I was supposed to pay sixty dollars to the company, that meant I have only made ten dollars for working somewhere between ten to fifteen hours that day. In essence, one would have to make a lot of money so that there would be more to keep.

Luisah's big white house in Oakland, California was situated just at the border between Oakland and Berkeley. Numerous women of great beauty, grace, and elegance, and from various regions of Northern California converged on this massive 'white house' she called ILE ORUNMILA OSUN. She combined some of the tenets of Traditional Yoruba Religion with that of Santeria and Lucumi to evolve a new kind of traditional Yoruba religion that was feminist in outlook. The aim of their gathering was to venerate the Yoruba goddess of the river and of childbirth – Osun. The ironic thing about this was that the women were not looking for children from Osun at all. They were basically feminists. Luisah, who insisted she should be addressed as 'Iya', placed a huge sign at the entrance to the house, which read: TRUST IN GOD SHE WILL PROVIDE! To her, God was a woman. Usually, the women would be dressed in seductive white attires such as skirts and blouses, gowns, and any African looking attires, complete with flowery headgears, which of course looked as if they made them. The women murmured, chatted in low voices, giggled, and laughed hysterically when someone said something funny.

All these were a prelude to the real thing, which was the Osun worship for that evening. Omitolokun, a very light skinned African American man who was Iya's lead drummer came out in readiness for the upcoming Osun worship. I climbed up the stairs to the big living room and confronted him with many questions. First, why did he drop his American name for the Yoruba one – Omitolokun? He answered that he was an adherent of Yoruba Traditional Religion and that he did not want an English name he had before which was (Dexter James). He said that he wanted to shed all relics of the western world. He even said that he had thrown out all the forks, spoons, and knives in his house and that his family now eats with their fingers! Also, he said that in restaurants, people would be looking at his family in a most curious way as they dug into their dishes with their fingers and licking each finger after every morsel! Then Omitolokun said: "Oh! You must be the Nigerian playwright Iya has been talking about" I replied in the affirmative, and then he invited me to come and join his drumming group. I tried to excuse myself, but he insisted.

"You will play the drum with me today. You know if Iya sees a real Yoruba man handle the drum in such an essentially African way she would be delighted and possession would occur" Omitolokun insisted. "Possession… what kind of possession are you talking about I asked?" "Spiritual possession, of course, what is African traditional religion without spiritual possession? It has been a long time since Osun possessed any of these women and they are getting impatient. They want to feel the real thing. They want to reach the pinnacle of possession." He concluded. I began to think of Osun. I used to hear my father say that his mother was a priestess of Osun and that she was a popular one in Ogere, Ogun State of Nigeria. My father said that he used to be saddled with the responsibility of removing the seemingly countless leaves of *eko* that had been eaten by the Osun worshippers of Ogere. He used to tell me that he would run away, but his mother would say that whenever he returned from his 'prank' of running away, he must remove all the leaves from their premises for appropriate disposal. The Yoruba meal of *Eko* and *Akara* was a favourite of Osun worshippers. Then, in faraway America, I was being saddled with playing the drum for some American worshippers who must be possessed by Osun or they would all go home unhappy and unfulfilled. I could not fathom the idea and I thought definitely Omitolokun was trying to 'trap' me. What if I played and no one was possessed then they were likely to conclude that perhaps my drumming was inadequate in helping them to reach the level of possession? I looked straight at Omitolokun as he was setting the drums up in the big living room of the 'white house'. The other drummers were already filing in, some, with sandwiches in their hands and others munching on hamburgers and French fries. The worshippers stared at me.

Some greeted me and asked some questions about Yoruba culture, while others were simply excited to see me and to display their knowledge of Yoruba religion and culture. One particular one whose name was Sandra, but preferred to be called 'Osunwale' (which means the goddess of the river has come home), walked up to me and placed her arm around my neck. "I hear you are a playwright." She asked, smiling and placing some candies in her mouth. "Yes, I have written some plays," I replied. "Can you write one for Osun worshippers of Berkeley?" She asked again sitting down next to me and pushing the drum I was supposed to be playing away from me. A play for The Osun Worshippers of Berkeley; I actually wrote a play of that nature, later on, titled *The Mother of Secrets* which as of the time of this writing remained unpublished. "Can you teach me an Osun song?" She asked with her eyes sparkling, I thought she was a very beautiful woman except for the few strands of gray hair, which made her look a little older than her age. "Yes, I can teach you an Osun song" I replied.

"Owu ke Ela ke   *(The thread is long the wisdom is divine)*
Eni ma b'orisa sere o a b'imo jojo. *(One who will play with the goddess must have lots of children)*

E sa bi o	*(Who will have a child?)*
Emi (Refrain)	*(Me)*
Omo dudu yen	*(A child black and beautiful)*
Emi	*(Me)*
Omo rodo rodo	*(A child light skinned and handsome)*
Emi.	*(Me)*

"Wonderful, just wonderful Osunwale exclaimed, giving me a hug and dragging me to the middle of the great living room where other women were standing in clusters chatting and waiting for the grand entrance of 'Iya' and the eventual commencement of the Osun worship for that evening. Osunwale was singing as she approached the women "Owu ke, ela ke, eni ma b'orisa sere ... this is Dipo, a Nigerian playwright he has been teaching me a song about Osun. Dipo please sing the song; sing it, so they can learn it too." I looked around, then I saw a great long table to the right flank of the living room where fruits, cakes, pies, coffee, tea, and apple cider has been placed. Some women were standing by that table, ignoring what was going on in the middle of the room, but merely concentrating on their snacks of cake, coffee, and tea. "Yes, please, we love to hear the song. Hey, maybe you can teach Iya also?" One of the women, Osundele, replied as she toyed with the strands of her very long hair. She was definitely of American Indian descent as evidenced in her long jet black hair. Her African American features only made her exotically beautiful. I found myself staring at her and then, Osunwale, who thought that by now she owned me tugged at my shirt a cue for me to begin the training session. "Owu ke, ela ke, eni ma b'orisa sere ... " I concluded the training session and as I walked away, from the middle of the room, a blonde white woman who apparently had not changed her name to a Yoruba name (Cassandra) followed me to the drummers' area of the living room and sat down with us. "I want to learn how to play the drum" she concluded stroking the top of the drum Omitolokun had pushed towards me to play. The drum was a West African *Djembe*, probably from Mali or Senegal but purchased of course in one of the many authentic African musical instrument stores in the area, perhaps the one known as The International Store for African Percussion "Have you ever played the *djembe* before?" Omitolokun asked even as he ignored Cassandra, who was busy scouting the array of musical instruments and trying to see which one was not being taken so she could grab it and essentially 'gatecrash' into the drummers' group. Omitolokun was not keen on letting her into the group, but unfortunately, she found one of the instruments – a *sekere,* whose player had not arrived that evening. She grabbed it. He was incensed, but said nothing. "Dipo, you will play the *djembe* for us this evening he continued as he played a couple of rhythms on his Conga drum. Some of the women swayed back and forth to the rhythm. The excitement level in the room shifted towards the drummers. There were women in front of us, beside us, and behind us. A few women ignored the excitement created by the drumming and stood by the snack table sipping coffee, laughing and giggling. I had asked Iya on one occasion why he named his house ILE ORUNMILA OSUN. She answered that her husband was a student of Ifa the traditional Yoruba divination system of which Orunmila is the patron god and that it was necessary to combine Osun and Orunmila in their 'Yoruba church'. Those who wanted to learn about Orunmila and the Ifa system of divination would go to her husband David Wilson, and those who wanted to learn about Osun would come to her, hence the name 'Ile Orunmila Osun'. It was around this time that David Wilson began to say these Yoruba words to me: "*Omo awo Olomi tutu*". Literally, the words mean "a member of a secret cult and owner of cold water"! I asked him whether he knew what the words meant, but he just laughed and said he did not know. I then told him the literal meaning of the Yoruba phrase and also told him that the words did not make any sense to me. That did not stop him from calling himself "*Omo awo olomi tutu*"!

The noise in the room was getting louder. It was a combination of rehearsal drumming, loud conversation, and laughter. Omitolokun looked at the time and it was about 6 p.m. He knew it was time to usher in 'Iya' herself. The routine for doing this was standard. He must first ward off the antics of the Yoruba god of trickery, the crossroads and of mischief - Esu. The drummers scrambled into position and upon the cue of the African gong player, the women began to sing in anticipation of Iya's entrance.

"Echu o elegbara ye   (Esu the powerful one please)
Echu o elegbara ye   (Esu the powerful one please)
Elegbara mo f'ori bale f'echu odara o. (The powerful one I bow
down before you)
Abo kenken abo kenken elegbara mo dupe (Protection please the
powerful one I thank you)

Abo kenken abo kenken." (Protection please protection please)

In this song, I recognized some Yoruba words. The drumming intensified. I saw some women swinging their long hair in circles, others dancing on their toes like ballerinas, while some were merely swinging from side to side with their eyes closed. Then to my surprise, they began to sing another song:

"Ibarapa o mo yuba*   (People of Ibarapa I pay homage)
Ibarapa o aye mo yuba (People of Ibarapa I pay homage)
E o w'Elegabra Ibarapa o aye mo yuba (Oh! Look at Esu, the god
of the crossroads People of Ibarapa I pay homage)
Elegbara mo yuba"   (The god of the crossroads I pay homage)

> I was surprised to note that they had a good knowledge of the Yoruba language to be able to sing a song in Yoruba.

*(However, I noticed that they could not pronounce the word 'juba' instead they pronounced the 'j' in the word like a 'y' making it sound like 'yuba'. Hence, the line 'Ibarapa o mo juba' would be 'Ibarapa o mo yuba'!)

ILE ORUNMILA OSHUN was conveniently converted into a 'church' a kind of religious edifice which guaranteed them an economic advantage – a tax-free status of a religious organization. I found it quite interesting that two Americans would value Yoruba traditional religion so much that they would turn their own house into the shrine of a Yoruba goddess – Osun. A lot of women came to the North Oakland mansion for a session of singing, dancing, and veneration of the goddess Osun. Everything took place in the big backyard. Even, the animal sacrifices of a rooster or the like took place there. It was a marvel to see all of these in a place called Oakland, California, in the United States.
Another song of the worshippers went like this:

"Ogu* re arere ile gbogbo l'Ogu wa
Ogu wa lule Ogu wa lona
Ibi gbogbo l'Ogu wa e"

*Ogu (More appropriately, 'Ogun', in the Yoruba language, is the god of hunters, blacksmiths, metals, war, and the road, often depicted as brave, volatile, restive and with a penchant for blood.) "I translated this one as:

We have seen Ogun.
Ogun is everywhere.
Ogun is at home Ogun is on the road.
Ogun is everywhere".

Ile Orunmila Oshun put out many newsletters, informing the public about their activities. I found the one they put out in February 1985, quite striking. Incidentally, it was that same year that Luisah Teish's book *Jambalaya The Natural Woman's Book of Personal Charms and Practical Rituals* came out from Harper and Row Publishers. The February 1985 calendar carried the following information:

In February 1985, Ile Orunmila Oshun was incorporated as a church of the Yoruba Religion under the leadership of Luisah Teish, James Bode Fasuyi, and David Wilson. We now have a non-profit status. The church is located at 1026 53rd St. Oakland, California. 94608. Teish's book, Jambalaya: The Natural Woman's Book of Personal Charms and Practical Rituals, published by Harper and Row, San Francisco, is now available at your local bookstores. Book parties and public readings and rituals have been scheduled. Watch for book reviews and interviews in The Wise Woman Newsletter, Shaman's Drum Magazine, and your local newspaper." (ILE ORUNMILA OSHUN NEWSLETTER Feb. 1985).

Apart from the announcement of the Ile Orunmila Oshun as a church, and the regular book reviews that were slated to follow the release of the book by Harper and Row, I was captivated by the announcement concerning "the rituals" that were supposed to follow the public readings. It was clear that the readings presented an avenue to further Luisah's ritual as engendered in her Oshun worship. I thought that was quite brilliant; a reading from a book about spirituality for women, followed by female rituals of "personal charms and practical rituals." I thought that a prospective audience member at such a reading would be getting "two for the price of one" so to speak, and that was likely to encourage that audience member to purchase the book and become a member of Ile Orunmila Oshun. I did not ask her if the rituals at the readings were recruitment drives, but it crossed my mind at the time, as it seemed that after the publication of the book, the membership of Ile Orunmila Oshun increased tremendously. Still, on the calendar of February 1985, it is necessary to review other entries that I found interesting. The following, from The Calendar, concerned the classes at Ile Orunmila Oshun:

1. *Circle One Members: Iya will begin classes on Dida Obi the first week of December.*
2. *Circle Three Members: Please accept my apology for neglecting to start the introductory classes on African Goddesses as promised in the last newsletter, It's been a heavy fall season. These classes have been postponed until March.*
3. *Yoruba Drama Workshop call Dipo at 658-4220.*
4. *Yoruba theology classes, call Omo Lawo David G. Wilson 654-8644.*
5. *The Yoruba Language call Adebisi Y. Aromolaran 428- 2268.*
   (ILE ORUNMILA OSHUN
NEWSLETTER Feb. 1985).

Number three above concerned the classes on Yoruba Drama that I had spoken to Luisah about. My name and phone number were therefore included in the list of Instructors at Ile Orunmila Oshun. I was interested in offering the drama classes as I thought that ritual or religion was very close to drama and that since the members of The Church were already indoctrinated into the rituals concerning Oshun, I could begin to intimate them with the rudiments of what I referred to as "Yoruba Drama." Really, Yoruba Drama was not a drama written or performed in the Yoruba language, but a drama that was written by a Yoruba dramatist infused for example, with Yoruba idioms, nuances, philosophy, religion, rituals, morals and ethics. I was a firm believer in the fact that Yoruba dramatists writing in English may be misunderstood if the Yoruba nuances of their dramatic composition were not properly addressed. My time at *The Black Repertory Theatre* reinforced this belief. A theatre director there had turned down directing my play – *The Graduate Palava* because it was too "African". Eventually, I had to direct the play myself.

I began the Yoruba Drama classes at Ile Orunmila Oshun with some of the plays of these female Ghanaian playwrights Ama Ata Aidoo, and Efua Sutherland. In the case of Ama Ata Aidoo, I picked her play – *The Dilemma of a Ghost* a play about the marriage between a Ghanaian man, Ato Yawsen, and an African American woman- Eulalie. I tried to show the aspects of African culture and philosophy inherent in the play and the fact that, in the African society, marriage between a man and a woman is a communal affair. It was not the individualistic "me and my wife" syndrome of the western world. As for Efua Sutherland's play, I picked *The Marriage of Anansewa,* which was a play based on the Ghanaian folk opera tradition of the "cunning tortoise" prevalent in African folktales. Ananse, the old father of Anansewa had promised his daughter to four men simultaneously, in order to extort money and gifts from all of them. In the end, it was the 'good' chief who finally married Anansewa despite Ananse's overt cunningness. Again, I tried to show the prevalence of African culture in the play and the fact that marriage in the African society was indeed an aspect of its complex culture. Finally, I tried to adapt the story of *Moremi* the Yoruba folkloric heroine, who pledged the life of her only child – Oluorogbo, to the River Goddess Esinmirin for the safe deliverance of the people of Ile Ife from the constant wars and enslavement the people of Igbo, or (Ugbo?), inflicted upon them. Moremi allowed the enemy to capture her and she became the wife of the king of Igbo**. It was when she was there that she extracted the secret of the Igbo people from their king, and sneaked back to Ile Ife. The next time the Igbo people came to wage war on Ile Ife, they were defeated.

** Igbo: *The people of Ibo land in Nigeria are known as Igbo (variably, Ibo). They mostly inhabit the South Eastern part of present day Nigeria. One version of the folklore suggests that the people of Ile Ife were constantly attacked, and sometimes enslaved, by the people of Igbo, who used their masquerades clad in dry raffia skirts and masks to terrorize the people of Ile Ife. However, there is 'Ugbo' which is a town in Yoruba land that may more appropriately fit the town mentioned in the Moremi folklore. The people of 'Ugbo' in Yoruba land through their King Olugbo of Ugboland claim that they were the original inhabitants of Ile Ife and that they had been driven away by Oduduwa who became the king of Ile Ife. It was from Ugboland then, that the people of 'Ugbo' came as masquerades in raffia skirts and masks to attack the people of Ife.*

> *Duro Ladipo's dramatization of the folklore/myth shows characters such as Igbo King, and Dibia, the latter in our present time, is the approximate equivalent of an Ifa Priest or a Babalawo, among the Yoruba people. If we are to go by his electrifying dramatization of the myth, it would seem that the people of "Igbo" (Ibos) were the ones who constantly terrorized the people of Ile Ife. I know that there are two accounts of this myth, but in Nigeria, Ladipo's dramatic presentation of the myth has remained the most classic, authoritative, and enthralling.*

I tried to show the workshop participants the importance of women in the society and the fact that a folkloric heroine like Moremi was able to free Ile Ife from the atrocities of the people who waged war on the people of Ile Ife and terrorized them constantly. In my workshop presentation, I noticed that the participants were more interested in this play based on the famous Yoruba folktale of Moremi, more than the plays of Aidoo and Sutherland. I ended up teaching them songs from the play I knew from the Duro Ladipo production of the play in Nigeria. One of them was '*Ere ka re 'le mi o*' (Profits come home with me), apparently a song that was sung by market women before an apparent vicious attack from the enemy. The other one was '*Moremi Ajasoro,*' (Moremi, one who uses fighting as her secret cult). Because of the popularity of the workshop scenes from *Moremi*, one of the participants, Sandra, asked me for permission to change her name to Moremi. I laughed and told her that the name was not my property and that she was free to change her name to Moremi if she wanted. That same week, Sandra was called Moremi by everyone.

I had a rollicking time with the participants in my drama classes which I held in the backyard of the house. I used to refer to the space where the classes took place as "The Courtyard Theatre". The participants, for obvious reasons, appreciated the ritualistic element of the play.

They pestered me about producing one of my plays at The Church, but I told them that "The Courtyard Theatre" was inadequate for a stage presentation and that we were likely to disturb the neighbours with the noise of a stage production involving music and dance.

Number four in the calendar was, of course, the Yoruba Theology classes offered by Luisah's husband – David Wilson. He is the one referred to as *Omo Lawo*. Really in the usual Yoruba parlance, *Omo Lawo* should have been *Omo Awo*, which means a neophyte in a certain mystery or secret cult. In essence, then, David was at the initial stage of his Ifa study and perhaps, at the time, he should not have been offering classes on the knowledge he was still acquiring. The item on the calendar even stated that he would be offering classes on "Yoruba Theology" which, again, is a deep-rooted mystical phenomenon requiring a long apprenticeship and practice. In 1985, I was sure that he had not acquired the long apprenticeship I mentioned as he was referred to as "*Omo Lawo*" that is, a learner. Number five on the calendar of classes concerned the actual Yoruba language classes of Adebisi Y. Aromolaran. He was an erudite person who had been popular in Nigeria, as a great exponent of the Yoruba language. He had been noteworthy for the *Akomolede Ijinle Yoruba* language series, Published by Macmillan, London. It was also offered in Nigeria, by the Onibonje Press. Akomolede really means one who teaches a child the language, in this case, the Yoruba language. The whole title really means "One who teaches a child the original Yoruba language" His books had been widely used in primary schools in Nigeria as part of the standard Yoruba language text... He had moved to the San Francisco Bay area, opening up a bookshop in Berkeley known as *The African Book Mart*. This individual then was well qualified to handle the Yoruba language classes listed in the calendar.

The next item on the calendar that was of interest to me was subtitled as Rituals in this way:

1. November 28th (Thanksgiving) There will be an Abundance Ritual in celebration of Indian Harvest. 8 pm at The Church. Bring abundance symbols for the altar, food, and drink to share and a candle (Brown, orange, green, or yellow). Donation
2. December 4th is the traditional feast of *Chango**, the Lord of the Flame. There is no formal ceremony at the church, but this is the time to bring offerings of apples, red peppers, and honey to *Chango's* shrine, and to pray for courage, justice, and the death of sexism. Burn red and white candles. Readings from Ifa are available. Call Babalawo Fasuyi 654-4220. Tarot and Coco readings call Teish 654-8644. The Church is now prepared to perform naming ceremonies, hand fasting, weddings, first menses ritual, manhood and wise

woman rituals, memorials, and other rites of passage. These
may be tailored to meet individual needs. *ACHE* (ILE
ORUNMILA OSHUN NEWSLETTER Feb. 1985).
*(*Chango* should be more appropriately **Sango** in the Yoruba
language)

Considering the two items above, the celebration of Indian Harvest
in a ritual manner is striking, since Thanksgiving, as observed in the
United States, has everything to do with the American Indians
(referred to in the piece above as "Indian"). As part of the history
and myth go, when the founding fathers of America, William
Bradford, and the Mayflower Pilgrims, arrived in 1619 at Plymouth
Rock in New England, they were ignorant about what to plant, and
which vegetables were safe to eat. Apparently, they starved during
that first year of their arrival, ignorant of how to grow basic food
items such as corn, potatoes, lettuce, cabbage, sweet potatoes and
the like. It was the American Indians, they found in the land that
showed them how to grow, what to grow, and when to harvest. The
second year they had a bountiful harvest, and since then
Thanksgiving had been celebrated in the United States as a time to
give thanks and as a holiday. It was the ritual element of the
celebration of the harvest that caught my attention, and the fact that
Luisah's ritual and religion, even celebrated The American Indians,
and their contribution to the development of the United States
agricultural and political superpower. To me, the ritual reminded
me of the new yam festival in Yoruba land which occurred in the
month of August every year. That ritual or festival is quite elaborate
and the sitting Yoruba king of the particular town must be the first
to eat the new yam.

Number two in the piece above concerned the Yoruba god of
thunder and lightning – Sango, referred to in the calendar as
"*Chango*." It was interesting to note that one of the offerings Luisah
required for the worship of Sango was red peppers. Traditionally,
anything red could be used to venerate the god. Since red pepper is
'hot' and Sango has a fiery (hot) temper, the item seemed
appropriate. The worshippers were also to pray for courage, an

attribute which Sango has in abundance. In terms of justice and the death of sexism, I was at a loss as to how these fit into Sango's attributes. The idea of "the death of sexism" only reminded me of the fact that it was part of the philosophy of the worshippers. I did not think that Sango was aware of "sexism". As for 'justice' within the Yoruba worldview, it was the exclusive preserve of a combination of forces: *Esu*, the trickster god, the god of the crossroads, and the policeman of God, *Oro* – the secret cult of retributive justice, and the *Ogboni* secret cult, who helped in the traditional administration of justice. At any rate, Sango would have been too fiery tempered to be involved in the administration of any 'justice'. His often rash actions have been justice enough!

The rituals concerning the rites of passage were very catching. Part of it seemed like the ones I was familiar with, for example, naming ceremonies, weddings, and the rite of passage into manhood. In Yoruba land, these would be elaborate rituals which may vary from place to place, but the objective of the rituals would be the same. I did not witness any of these rituals while I was at the Ile Orunmila Oshun, but the fact they were listed in the calendar suggested Luisah's thoroughness as a Priestess of Oshun.

In the note following number two above, worshippers were urged to patronize Babalawo

Bode Fasuyi, who was the authentic Babalawo from Nigeria that Luisah accommodated at Ile Orunmila Oshun. This was a plus for The Church because it made the worshippers actually patronize this Babalawo. They used to come in large numbers to seek his services. Sometimes they would meet me at home greet me only passingly, and walk down to the basement where Fasuyi also lived. His basement apartment was directly opposite my own. In order to satisfy my curiosity, I would sit in on some of the Ifa readings that Fasuyi conducted for some of his clients. Essentially, Fasuyi and I became friends, and he used to joke that it seemed that I was trying to become a Babalawo (an Ifa priest) as well as a playwright. I told him that the mystery of Ifa was actually in my family. He did not believe me and he asked me to tell him how I knew that Ifa was in my family. This was what I told him.

When I was first coming to the United States in 1971, my mother took me to go and see a Babalawo in Ogere, my father's town. The name of the Babalawo was *Olugbiyen*. He was my uncle (my father's brother). My mother wanted him to consult Ifa on my behalf so that we would know something about my impending journey to the United States. Olugbiyen then told me that an Ifa Priest, or a Babalawo, whose name was *Lemolu,* was the founder of our town and that he was also a Babalawo. He said that he had come from Ile Ife with a brother and that when he reached the spot where Ogere is today, he consulted his Ifa oracle, and the oracle told him that he should settle on that spot. Olugbiyen then said that all the paraphernalia of Ifa that Lemolu used was still in our family home at *Ita Jinren* in Ogere.

Another story was from my elder brother, Tunde. He was a student of Mechanical Engineering in the United Kingdom sometime in the early 1970s. He said that on a snowy, windy day in London, he had just stepped out of his apartment to go out when he met a white man who looked a lot older than him. He said the man told him that there was a very important god in our ancestry and the god had been there a long time, but unfortunately, it had been neglected. The white man then told my brother that the god had been neglected, and that it was "hungry" and needed to be fed, and that if that was not done, people in the family would die! Tunde wrote our father who was in Nigeria and inquired about what the white man said. Our father had to admit to him that the corpus of Ifa was in our family and that the paraphernalia for Ifa divination was still in our ancestral home in Ogere. A lot of sacrifices had to be made to placate Orunmila – the god of divination. My father, having converted to Christianity at that time merely asked his younger brother in Ogere to take care of the atonement.

Fasuyi believed my stories, but insisted that I was not an initiate of Ifa, and he was not going to teach me about the mystery. I told him that since we have the mystery in our family, I do not need him to teach me, and then we laughed about the whole affair.

Luisah Teish was kind enough to give me an autographed copy of her book- *Jambalaya*. In the book, she wrote:

"To my man Dipo: We have come and gone a long way together. Your approval represents passing the acid test; and if you understand the crazy warp of Black Americans a little better, then my work has been well done.
In Woman Spirit Iya, Nov. 1985. Teish"

She was right about the fact that "we have come a long way together" because I actually met her in 1976, during my undergraduate days at the University of California at Berkeley. I thought that what she meant about the "crazy warp of Black Americans" merely meant the mixture of African American with white American culture and in fact other cultures in the American diaspora. For example, it was not impossible to see Black Americans that were mixtures of white, American Indians, Scottish, German, and Swiss! I actually enjoyed reading *Jambalaya* despite the fact that it was designed for women's spirituality. I read the book several times, making so many notes in pencil, that when I picked up the book recently, I was amazed that I had pencilled notes on virtually every page! I know that if I embark upon a critical analysis of the book here, it would derail the spirit of this memoir that I am trying to establish. At any rate, a few comments about the book will be in order, especially, since my notes in pencil are still clearly visible. In the preface of the book, Luisah claims that:

The women's movement has worked to reclaim the women's knowledge and power. This quest has led to a rejection of patriarchal religion and the rebirth of nature – centered Woman Spirit movement. We have learned the true definition of words, which have, in the past, been shrouded in fear and perverted by misinterpretation. Words such as witch have been redefined in the light of their true origin and nature. Instead of the evil, dried out, old prude of patriarchal lore, we know the witch to be a strong, proud woman, wise in the ways of natural medicine. We know her as a self-confident freedom fighter, defending her right to her own sexuality, and her right to govern her life and community according to the laws of nature. We know that she was slandered, oppressed, and burned alive for her wisdom and her defiance of patriarchal rule. (*Jambalaya* ix)

This opening salvo registers her disaffection for "patriarchal religion". But what is a patriarchal religion? It seems that "knowledge and power" have something to do with what she refers to as "patriarchal religion". So, the caveat about religion is really about who controls this "knowledge and power". This is where the concept of witchcraft evolves. Some people believe that a witch is someone who attains the pinnacle of knowledge. In Yoruba land, for example, some people refer to "witches" as "*awon t'ogbon*", that is, "those who have the knowledge, out of fear of saying the actual Yoruba word for a witch- *aje*. However, the "knowledge" they refer to here is not just ordinary physical knowledge about a subject. It is mystical knowledge tied to the very cryptic essence of natural law. The concept of the Yoruba cosmos being saturated with mystery comes to mind. The cosmos that boasts of a continuum of the dead, the ancestors, the unborn, and the living, juxtaposed in one unbroken cycle of existence is enigmatic at best. It is only "those who have knowledge" that can unravel knowledge from the vortex of this cryptic abyss. Now, women are usually associated with witchcraft. If this assertion holds, then it follows that women "have knowledge" and are, therefore "wise", that is "*awon t'ogbon*." Again, if this holds as well, it stands to reason that women have an edge over men in this regard. In the Yoruba culture, the concept of witchcraft imbibes the good and the bad in the witch. That is, the knowledge of witchcraft could be used for good or evil, however, it is the evil that seems to get the greatest publicity.

For example, when a witch kills the child of her neighbour in Yoruba land, it would be more news than if the same witch used her witchcraft to make her son wealthy. As journalists say "If it bleeds; it leads."

I told Luisah that her concept of the witch had all the connotations of the western world. For example, when she mentioned "burned alive for her wisdom" in the piece above, what came to my mind was the infamous Salem witch hunt of Massachusetts New England, in 1692 and 1693, where women accused of witchcraft were actually burned to death. I see religion first and foremost as a mystery. The book, according to Luisah, "Concentrates on the Voudou of New Orleans, and that it is like Jambalaya, a spicy dish with many fine ingredients cooked together. It blends the practices of three continents into one tradition. It contains African ancestor reverence, Native American earth worship, and European Christian occultism."

(*Jambalaya* x.) In the light of this, my fascination with the book was mainly the African (Yoruba spirituality) as it was the one in which I was familiar with. The following also captivated me:

"The book is written under the guidance of "She Who Whispers," my spirit-guide, as a contribution to our healing. It is written specifically for women. It lifts the heavy skirts of God the Mother and proudly displays the fruit of Her womb. The Voudou has special appeal to women. Because it is the child of matristic traditions, it recognizes spiritual kinship; encourages spiritual growth; respects the earth; and utilizes the power of sexuality and women's menstrual blood. Menstrual taboos that were originally holy and self- imposed have become accursed and oppressive under homophobic male domination. Menstrual blood can be used to control men, but as feminists – spiritualists, we have better things to do with it. Unfortunately, many women are still afraid of their

natural essence, the Voudou will help them to overcome this fear".
(*Jambalaya* x-xi)

From the above, Luisah believes that mystery is female, but the mystery, the essence of "God", has no gender. She refers to this essence as "She who Whispers", and "God the Mother". I took her up on this idea after I must have read the book at least three times. But the entity we refer to as "God" is also, neither male nor female contrary to the sign she hung in her ILE ORUNMILA OSHUN which read: TRUST IN GOD SHE WILL PROVIDE. That entity is at best a conundrum, a spiritual essence. Her submission about the female menstrual blood was interesting to me in the sense that in Yoruba land, if a woman was to use her menstrual blood for evil purposes or "to control men", then that would be referred to as *juju*.

Incidentally, my own published plays *Polygyny and Polyandry: Two Plays about Marriage* were released by Macmillan Publishers London, in 1985. I gave Luisah a copy of the plays, as an exchange gesture to her, for giving me a copy of *Jambalaya*.

Bode Fasuyi had been pestering me about going to the house of a real American *Babalawo*. I had resisted his offer by telling him that the real Babalawo or priests of Ifa were in Yoruba land not far away America. Then he shoved *The East Bay Express* in my face saying: "read this". It was an elaborate interview and write up on one Guillermo Gonzalez, who was from Cuba, but living in East Oakland. A part of the write up was so fascinating to me. This was it:

I am a Cuban, I am a Latin American, and I am going to remain that till the day I die. Part of keeping that is to delve into my Cuban culture" Santeria, which he calls Regia Ocha (Rule of the Orisha) is an integral part of that heritage. Baptized Catholic, he rarely went to mass while growing up in New York City, and New Jersey. Like all Cubans, he says he knew about Santeria. His aunt set out red apparels and wine as offerings to Shango. Only as a college

student, when he began to sense the presence of the Orisha, did he become interested in Santeria. At thirty, he was initiated and received Yemaya, the goddess of the sea and fertility as his ruling Orisha. Gonzalez is eager to discuss the week long initiation during which he becomes a Santero, or a Priest. He has lived in Nigeria and extensively studied Ifa, the Yoruba tradition, in its purest form. We ask him first to explain the relationship of Ifa to its Latin American offspring. He says: Ifa is the cornerstone upon which everything else rests. Ifa is the source. It is not just a religion, it is a way of life, a way of truth, its theology, its morals, its philosophy, its ethics, its medicine, and it's therapeutic. It is as valid and as meaningful in terms of the human condition. As any of the world's great ways of truth, whether it be Islam, Christianity, or the way of our Hebrew brothers and sisters."
(*The East Bay Express June* 29,
1985).

When I read this interview/write up about Babalawo Fawoye, I was impressed. I thought my trip to his house would not be a waste after all. Imagine an American Babalawo who believed that: "Ifa is the cornerstone upon which everything else rests. Ifa is the source. It is not just a religion, it is a way of life, a way of truth, its theology, its morals, its philosophy, its ethics, its medicine, and it's therapeutic". I thought the visit was worth a trial.

Fasuyi and I went to Fawoye's house one hot, muggy, summer afternoon. I was surprised to note that there were many clients waiting by the door that leads to his house. He lived in the downstairs apartment of a fairly big house. I hesitated to go into his apartment, but Fasuyi persisted that I must follow him to meet this man. When I entered his apartment, I found out that it was neat and beautifully furnished. There were impressive paintings and sculptures of various Yoruba gods and goddesses on the walls, on the floor and even in the restroom! Obviously, that was a man who had a great love for Yoruba art, religion, and culture. A provocative sculpture of Osun with a big bust and a seductive smile stared one in the face as soon as one entered his living room. Of course, the impressive god of thunder, Sango, holding his trademark double headed axe was on the opposite side of the seductive Osun. Fawoye was seated on the floor. He was dressed in a flowing white *agbada*. To me, the *agbada* looked pseudo-Yoruba, because it has been modified somehow, I presume, for ease of free movement. He wore a white cap and his perennial smile seemed infectious. He held a divining chain, and a strikingly beautiful woman somewhere from the opulent Marin County in Northern California was seated in front of her. It seemed to me that the woman was there for a consultation with the Ifa Oracle. Fawoye eyed me somehow coyly and then smiled again.

"Baba, this is the Nigerian Playwright I promised to bring to see you," Fasuyi said with a kind of satisfaction I did not understand.

"Oh! Good afternoon … *Se dada ni*? Fawoye said as he tried to impress me with his little knowledge of the Yoruba language.

"Fasuyi is my good friend. He has told me a lot about you, your plays at the Black Repertory Theatre… I hear you have written a lot of plays. Have you written any one about Ifa? I answered that I had written some plays and that one of them was about Ifa. I neglected to tell him that the particular one about Ifa, *The Father of Secrets*, was really a satire on an Ifa Priest who was a charlatan!

"Thank you. Good afternoon. I hope you are well" I replied. Fasuyi wanted to make me see how important the Yoruba religion was in the United States and that there were real people who were Americans, but deeply rooted in the Yoruba culture even more than the Yoruba people back in Nigeria. Fasuyi looked at Fawoye with respect and admiration and looked at me with a sort of "I told you so" countenance. I had argued with him several times about his submission, that is, that I did not believe him. Of course, in front of me was Guillermo Gonzalez, an African American man who had converted to the Yoruba religion of the worship of Orunmila, (Ifa), and who had changed his name to Baba *Fawoye*.

"Please sit down… sit down". Baba Fawoye ordered. Fasuyi and I looked at ourselves and the sofa to the right, and we sat down.

Fasuyi kept whispering to me all the time we were there that
Fawoye was the most popular Babalawo in East Oakland and that
people came from far away places to ask him to consult the Ifa
Oracle on their behalf. He even said that Native Americans came to
Baba Fawoye as well.

"You will excuse me while I hold consultations with the Ifa Oracle
on behalf of Maggie," Fawoye said as he grabbed his divining chain
and threw it on the divining tray pushing it back and forth and
mumbling some Ifa verses. I wanted to hear the verses in Yoruba,
but he could only speak minimal Yoruba so that the rest of the
verses he could not say in the Yoruba language he rendered in
English. I was a bit taken aback as I knew the power of the
language. To me, the Yoruba language is so cryptic it almost defies
translation, and even then when one succeeds in translating it into
English, the nuances, tonality, pun, satire, philosophy, and even
sound would likely be lost. I listened to Baba Fawoye's rendition of
the Ifa verses. He was even adept at saying the *Iyere Ifa,* the part of
the Oracle that is always musical and incantatory in nature. In fact,
a good mark of an Ifa Priest is the person's ability to recite or sing
the *Iyere Ifa,* which goes with the actual ifa verse concerning the
problem at hand. Incidentally, every Ifa verse has its own peculiar
Iyere Ifa. "Maggie" Baba Fawoye, called the lady in his quiet husky
voice. I could not imagine such a large man with a soft voice like
that. "Ifa says that you have to allow your inner head freedom to
make you become what you are destined to become". He paused
and looked at Maggie intently. Maggie seemed puzzled as she
stroked her hair and placed another chewing gum in her mouth.
"Inner head?" Maggie asked. "But Baba, what is an inner head?"
"Maggie", Baba Fawoye continued. "The Yoruba people believe
that every individual has an "inner head" and an "outer head". They
also believe that each individual has a guiding Orisha; the one that
guides your inner head. The inner head is your spirit, your destiny,
while the outer head is the physical head we see every day." He
paused for effect as he pushed the divining chain back and forth.
"So Baba what you are telling me is that I have two heads." He

suppressed a laugh and said, speaking slowly and intently as before like a school teacher giving instruction to a student. "Yes, we all have two heads. In fact, the inner head is the fate or destiny you brought from Olodumare, that is, God. That fate or destiny is housed in your inner head. You will need to placate your head... your inner head that is so that everything you want in life would come to you. Right now, your inner head is not very happy with you." But Baba, another reason I came to you is that my boyfriend left me and ran away to Washington, D.C. Look, Baba, I did not do anything bad to him... he just got up and left... just like that, saying that he was tired of me, that I was too persistent.. Can you believe that Baba? My own boyfriend telling me he is tired of me?" Baba Fawoye looked at her and answered this way: "Placate your inner head".

"And I am looking for a job and I don't seem to have any luck. Lots of interviews but no offer of a job" Baba Fawoye merely answered that she should placate her inner head. Then he said: "You must offer sacrifices. Your guiding god is Ogun- the Yoruba god of iron, war, hunters, and everything that has to do with metal or iron. Ogun is angry that you have not offered sacrifices to him. Ogun is hungry. If you offer sacrifices to him, then he would clear the way for you. Ogun is the path clearer. Your way will be smooth. Your problems will disappear." Maggie looked at Baba Fawoye for a while and then spoke. "So what are the items for this sacrifice to Ogun?" Baba Fawoye answered even as he sang the *Iyere Ifa* concerning the Ifa verse that came out of the Ifa corpus. You will offer a dog, palm wine, kola nuts... lots of kola nuts, yam flour, and ram meat." I kept looking at Fasuyi who had brought me to see Baba Fawoye. Fasuyi was pleased that he was conducting the business of Ifa in such an orthodox way. He even told me that Baba Fawoye had received some tutoring in Ifa from him, but that he would not admit that publicly. I wondered how Maggie would get palm wine. Then Maggie spoke. "Baba what would you do with the dog?" "I will cut off its head with one swift stroke of the machete to placate Ogun." "You mean you will kill the dog?" Baba Fawoye answered in the affirmative. Maggie was sad. She told him that she had a dog in Marin County where she lived and that its name was 'Whiskey'. She had named it 'Whiskey' because when she first got the dog and it was a puppy, it licked some of the whiskey she was drinking right from the cup she was holding. It was that incident that made her name the dog, a Siberian husky, – Whiskey. She said that she loved Whiskey so much and she would not think of killing whiskey for Ogun. Baba Fawoye told her that he would not have to kill Whiskey, but another dog to which she had no emotional attachment. The thought of killing any dog was unbearable for Maggie. I saw tears welling up in her eyes, and then she said "Baba, dogs are such lovely pets. They are better than human beings… really. They won't stab you in the back as humans do. Their love is unconditional, and they don't harbour grudges. Really, Baba are you really going to kill the dog as you have said?"

Fawoye did not seem to want to answer her question at that time. He felt that she was a neophyte who had to be eased in gradually into the mysterious ways of the Yoruba Orisha worship. He knew that she had been raised as a Christian, of the Episcopalian persuasion, and that frustration and disenchantment with the Episcopalian Church drove her to embrace Yoruba Orisha worship.

Still, she insisted that she would rather not be responsible for the death of a dog. She said that would be cruel. Then she asked where and how Baba Fawoye would kill the dog. He told her that in his backyard, in the dead of night about 2. A.m., and it would be with a swift stroke of a very sharp machete. He told her that if he had to kill the dog with more than one stroke of the machete, then the sacrifice would not be acceptable to Ogun. "There is a warrior instinct in you. That is why Ogun is your guiding Orisha. You never give up, you fall down, but you get up and keep trying. You are also a restless person, like your god – Ogun. Passivity bores you. You must be active all the time, just like Ogun." Baba concluded, smiling at her and happy about the revelation about her that he had received from Ifa. "Wow! You know Baba; you are so right about that. You are just so right." She admitted.   Baba

Fawoye continued to persuade her for a while about the importance of the sacrifice. The session ended with Baba promising to take care of the sacrificial items if she would pay for them. She reluctantly agreed to pay, but up till the time she left Baba Faowye's residence, she continued to beg him not to kill any dog because of her problems.

When we left Baba Fawoye's house, I asked Fasuyi what he thought of our visit. He was full of praises for Baba Fawoye. He thought he was a man who was not ashamed of his roots – his African roots. He said he took me to see him so that I can see that Yoruba Traditional Religion and culture were thriving in the United States and that it was only in Nigeria, Yoruba land in particular, where people were ashamed of their traditional religion, believing that it was fetish, and idol worship. I told him that I was already aware of the popularity of Yoruba religion in the American Diaspora and that I was impressed especially when Baba Fawoye was reciting the *iyere ifa.*

Not long after my visit to Baba Fawoye, I had to move out of Luisah Teish's house. Her worship of Osun and the fact that Luisah insisted that everyone should call her "Iya" was irritating my wife. My wife told me that she could not call her 'Iya' as she was African, Yoruba, and more in tune with the Yoruba culture, Luisah held so dearly and with such conviction. My wife even told me about her experience with the goddess – Oshun. She told me that when she was in the secondary school – Baptist High School Ede, in Nigeria, that she was a member of the school's dance troupe. She said that one day while the school was performing a dance in honour of Oshun; she became possessed and danced out of the hall where the event was taking place, towards the local river that was in the town. The Oshun worshippers thought she was one of them and saved her from jumping into the rather deep river. They had to carry out rituals and sacrifices to placate Oshun, who had apparently possessed my wife and was waiting for her to come and meet her in the river! When the sacrifices and rituals were completed and my wife was dragged away from the banks of the river, the Oshun priestesses could not believe that she was not an initiate of Oshun. They maintained that only an initiate could be possessed in the way Jumoke was possessed. Obviously, she could not swim and could have drowned in the river. Ironically, she had an intense phobia for any body of water. "You see I am more of an Oshun worshipper than she is" my wife quipped.

She did not tell Luisah this story. Jumoke looked at Luisah's Oshun worship with certain scepticism; however, Teish was intensely kind and generous to us. She became so friendly with my family and joked around that she was going to adopt one of our daughters – Olubukola, whom we affectionately called "Buki" for brevity. Of course, my wife would have none of that, but Teish's continued kindness and generosity, particularly towards Buki became a matter for jokes and laughter between my wife and me. One day, the postman brought a heavy cardboard box labelled "To Olubukola Kalejaiye". When we received the box, we were surprised as Buki was only about three years old at the time, and there was no way anyone would be mailing a huge parcel to her. We opened it and of course, Luisah had ordered colourful books and writing materials for Buki. We were impressed and we went upstairs to find her in the huge living room adjacent to her Oshun shrine, to thank her for the kind gesture.

When I began working as a cab driver for the Goodwill Cab Company, I was apprehensive about the arrangement. I was to keep all the proceeds from the cab driving on any given day except for sixty-eight dollars, which I must pay to the company as what they called "the gate". That was what the company must receive for loaning me the cab all day long, for about twelve to fifteen hours daily. I presumed at the time that the gate was for the maintenance of the cabs, and profit for the company. One day, the Dispatcher spoke to me in this manner:

308... come in 308. Yes. I said come in 308. What? What do you mean? You are breaking up 308. Look, 308... you are breaking up. 308, I am not going to put up with your bullshit today 308. I gave you a fare. No, don't tell me what I said. I know what I said. I gave you a fare. Yes. Pick up at Highland Psych. Yes, Highland Psych. Come back 308. What? I said Highland Psychiatric Hospital in Oakland. What the hell did you mean by that? What? You heard me. Yes, Highland Psychiatric Hospital. You mean you don't know where the Highland Psychiatric Hospital is anymore? Come on man. I'm getting tired of you this morning 308.

The Goodwill Cab Company was located on East Fourteenth Street in East Oakland California. It was at the entrance to the street as one approaches it from the downtown area. The gorgeous Lake Merritt, a haven for joggers and other health conscious fanatics, was only a short walking distance from the beginning of it.

The street was the *Apian Way*, which goes into the heart of East Oakland - that Godforsaken part of the city where prostitutes, drug dealers, drug users, and the mentally ill call home. That was the area of the city one could confidently refer to as a ghetto. Abandoned store fronts and houses dotted the long winding street which went all the way into San Leandro, a city which had many used car dealerships. The Street's trademark was run down houses which at the time were used as makeshift drug houses by drug dealers. Of course, whenever the police found out about the illicit operations the houses would be boarded up immediately. Drunken old men, miscreants, prostitutes, pimps, thieves, beggars, the jobless, gamblers, and street hawkers selling fake or stolen goods also called East Fourteenth Street home.

One day, on East Fourteenth, as I sat in my cab waiting for a fare in front of a famous grocery store- Lucky's, a young African American man of only about twenty walked up to me. I was happy I was going to pick up a fare and make some money. "Where are you going?" I asked, but he said he was not going anywhere but that he wanted to show me a brand new VCR which he had for sale. My wife and I had been talking about getting a VCR, but we could not afford it. "Yes, I will like a VCR," I said to the young man as I fixed my gaze on the scar on his forehead, which looked like it might have been from a knife wound. "Hey man, it's gonna be fifty dollars man… you got fifty dollars? I only had twenty-three dollars in my pocket that day and I told him so. After much haggling, the young man accepted twenty dollars. I kept the heavy VCR box in my cab and did not open it till I got home. It was when I got home that I found out that the carefully packaged "VCR" was only a box of stones wrapped neatly with a newspaper- *The San Francisco Chronicle*! My two daughters and my wife had so much fun laughing at my naiveté. They laughed till their sides ached.

In order to take their minds off making fun of me, I told them the story of my one month sojourn with Solomon Rasheed, which occurred when I was an undergraduate at The University of California at Berkeley. He was a vivacious, aggressive, and ironic fifty five-year-old African American man. He had given me part of what looked like an apartment in the back of a storefront facing East Fourteenth Street. It seemed as if he lived inside the storefront as there seemed to be a smaller studio apartment attached to the storefront.

He claimed that he was an African and that his father had forcibly brought him to the United States. His real name, of course, was not Solomon Rasheed but it seemed to me that he had largely dropped what he called his "slave name" for what he termed the more African – "Solomon Rasheed". I reminded him that the name "Solomon" was in the Bible and that it actually reminded me of King Solomon, who was the king of Israel, and the son of King David. He got upset with me and said that as far as he was concerned "Solomon" was an African name. After all, King Solomon was the son of the African Queen of Sheba!" The Queen of Sheba?" I asked rhetorically, and he answered that he knew what he was saying and that he meant The Queen of Sheba! Then, he told me that The Queen of Sheba was actually an African woman from Ijebu Ode, a Yoruba town in Nigeria, who had heard of the wealth and glory of King Solomon and who was determined to go and marry him. He then told me that it was that union that produced the ancestor of Haile Selassie 1 – the last Emperor of Ethiopia's three-thousand-year-old monarchy! Also, he told me that *The Rastafarians* were descendants of King Solomon He warned me to stop talking about the bible and that even Jesus Christ was not white, but black. He even asked me if I had heard of the painting of a Black Madonna and child located in a church in Cologne Germany! I answered him in the affirmative. He then told me that I must never think of Jesus, as a white man ever in my life. Solomon Rasheed could not tell who his father was or if he had relatives here in the United States. Also, he did not know from which African country he had been brought to the United States, but he was always dressed in a flowing African garment with a turban to match although he claimed that he was not a Moslem. I was always curious about his turban. He had, as it seemed to me at the time about one thousand turbans, and there was always a turban to match any flowing garment he wore on a particular day. I used to joke with him that his collection of turbans was a collectors' item and that we may have to open a museum for them! He was fiercely African in everything he did. He had twenty authentic African drums in his house, which he neither played nor let anyone touch. He insisted that I must wash the bathtub after I took a shower, and he did the same too. He was sort of a cleanliness freak and he would bend down to pick up a piece of paper that he saw on his approach to his tiny studio apartment. He did not have a wife, girlfriend, or children. In fact, he mentioned no family members or relatives to me, but there was always a woman, Ms. Corbin, who always visited him and he visited her. He would get upset if one was to refer to Ms. Corbin as his girlfriend, or that he was Ms. Corbin's boyfriend. He had no heat in his apartment, but would turn on the gas cooker, and open the oven so that the dry heat could come into the apartment and keep him warm. He was addicted to sugary meals, and candies were his favourite. He could eat a few packs of candy for breakfast and wash them down with strong black coffee. Ms. Corbin, his pseudo girlfriend, was like a mulatto, while Solomon Rasheed was extremely dark complexioned. My wife merely laughed and asked how I got entangled with such a strange character. I did not continue with the story of how I lived for a month with Solomon Rasheed because my wife had found it so funny, she was laughing as she did when I got deceived into buying a fake VCR.

Each cab of the Goodwill Cab Company was diligently numbered. For some reason, the cab I always ended up with was the one numbered "308". My journey that summer morning did not seem to be off to a good start. The taxi's radio made an annoying buzz as I swerved to avoid an oncoming trailer whose driver was blasting the horn in an exasperating manner. Then the trailer driver leaned out of the window and stuck out his middle finger at me in the familiar cursing fashion. I looked at him briefly even as his shirt flapped endlessly in the summer morning breeze. His trailer was a huge one with white, chrome showing on the rims of his tires and also on the side and rear panels. The hood covering the engine section was painted bright red with a picture of a blonde white woman sitting seductively on it. I thought about giving him a middle finger back, but instead, I got back on the road. As a cab driver, time is money and I wanted to make sure that I got back to the dispatcher. By getting back to the dispatcher he would at least know that I was available to be sent to pick up a fare. I picked up the microphone to call the taxi cab dispatcher.

I peered at the miscreants, drunks, and the "bold" prostitutes who dared to flaunt their "thing" at ten O'clock in the morning. One particular one, a strikingly beautiful African American woman of about twenty-three kept beckoning to me to pull over. To my shock, she bared her breast for me to see then quickly covered it up smiling seductively and beckoning to me to park my cab. I knew what she wanted; she did not need a cab. Another one, a white woman of about thirty or so, with long blonde hair and lipstick that was definitely overdone waved at me. She kept waving and walking as if her high heel shoes were quite uncomfortable. In fact, at a point, she removed them and continued to walk barefooted while still waving at me and wiggling her hips seductively. I was determined not to fall for that temptation. They seemed to forget that we were in search of the same thing – dollars for existence. I was not going to give them the proceeds from my cab-driving.

The buzzing sound of the microphone reminded me that I still had it in my hand. I called the dispatcher. "308 to dispatcher". There was no answer. I called again: "308 calling dispatcher." Still, there was no answer. "Dispatcher, this is 308 please come in". I heard a cough – yes, he coughed a lot. He was grossly overweight. There were silent rumours about the fact that he was a homosexual, but no one could provide any proof about that. All the cab drivers hated him because he was always rude, obnoxious, and often shouted obscenities at drivers. He was always in the habit of falling asleep in the cab office, right on his desk where all the gadgets for communications with the drivers were placed.

Once, I caught him actually drooling at the mouth. I had gone in to ask him a question and all I could do that day was just stand there and watch the flies swarm his drool with relish. Other flies made an all-you-can-eat buffet out of his half-eaten Macdonald's Big Mac and French fries. I knocked on the door to attract his attention or better still to wake him up but he just kept drooling. I marveled at the fact that he did not swallow up one of the flies or something of the sort. He hated questions; all sorts of questions automatically infuriated him. No driver dared to ask him directions to a particular location. He would scream and yell obscenities and tell the cab driver to go and look at his map. Yes, a map book was an invaluable tool all the drivers carried around yet, we were sometimes at a loss as to where a particular street or even a house on that street was located. The street would be perfectly visible on the map, but surprisingly unreachable or even non-existing in reality!

That day, drivers were struggling to reach him and cutting each other off over the air. We had to be fast in calling in to the dispatcher after we had dropped off our fares, especially, if we were free to pick up a new fare. Fastness equals a fare and a possibility that one would make some money. His name was Arthur Robinson. He wanted everyone to call him "Art" but I preferred the more formal "Arthur". I used to joke with him that his name reminded me of the fabled King Arthur. That did not stop him from being rude and obnoxious to me.

"308 to dispatcher." Yes, that was what we had to say. You called out (or yelled out) your cab number, and then add the words "to dispatcher." The reason for that was clear enough. That was the only way that the dispatcher could keep track of all the fifty-four cabs plying the streets at any given time. When I first started driving, I used to call out my name and then add the words "to dispatcher!" It didn't take long before I learned my lesson when I found out that he refused to acknowledge my radio call or send me to go and pick up a fare.

I called him on the radio again. "308 to Dispatcher!" He replied in his rude and obscene manner.

Shut the fuck up 308... what the hell is wrong with you? I said just a minute. Didn't you hear me say just a minute? Look, 308 you are pissing me off this morning. You just cut another driver off. What is your problem this morning 308? I ain't got time for your bullshit this morning. I mean it. If you don't feel like driving why don't you just bring the cab in, and take the day off. What the hell is the matter with you?"

I shuddered. A colleague who was quite popular as a journalist and drama reviewer for the *Nigerian Daily Times* back in the 1970s and 1980s in Nigeria, and who was also a "transplanted" Nigerian like me, Jide Osikomaiya, had complained of the rigours of cab driving to me. Just the previous week he had actually abandoned his cab in downtown Berkeley on University Avenue – somewhere near the

University of California at Berkeley. He swore never to try that kind of employment again, even if it meant he and his family of three were going to starve. I could not take such a step, besides; I knew it would not find favour with my wife.

I did not hear Arthur say "just a minute" but if I proceed to contest that issue, he would get more infuriated and perhaps go off radio communication with me for hours! That was the way he vented his anger. He would go off radio communication with any driver that angered him. I knew what that meant. He would not send me to pick up fares for hours. At the end of the day I would have no money to pay my sixty-eight dollars "gate" – the amount one must pay to the cab company every day at the end of one's shift. I waited. I was desperate. Unemployment had turned me into a cab driver. I was thinking of Jumoke my wife, and the three children. Before I became a cab driver, I had applied to so many community colleges and even universities, for a teaching position, but to my dismay, I only received rejection letters. Some of them would start like this:

"Thank you for applying for the position of Instructor at Diablo Valley College. Although we found your resume impressive we are sorry we could not offer you an appointment at this time. There were so many qualified candidates and the decision was not easy. We wish you success in your career options."

I became an expert in identifying a rejection letter. Once I opened it and it started with the words "Thank you…" I would immediately tear the letter and dispose of it without reading the rest of it.
"Yes 308… Come in 308".
I looked at the time it was about twelve noon. The dispatcher had calmed down somewhat and was ready to send me to go and pick up a fare.
"Yes, this is 308" I replied.

"Well, now 308... I'm glad you have now decided to listen instead of arguing with me. Now, pick up at "Highland Psych." The fare would be waiting at the entrance to the Emergency section of the hospital. Now, 308, this is a voucher fare. Just pick up the voucher from him. The government is paying. You know how that goes, right?"

My heart sank! We all hated the so-called 'voucher fares' especially, those at Oakland's Highland Psychiatric Hospital, which he often referred to as "Highland Psych." These were passengers who were on some kind of government assistance, and whose cab fares would be paid by the government. Usually, these clients did not tip, and they were unruly or downright rude. Some were definitely mentally ill and were cranky. Sometimes they would threaten cab drivers with bodily harm!

As soon as my cab pulled up to the front door of the hospital, I saw one of the nurses holding an African American man, in one hand and a slip of paper in another hand. I knew what the slip of paper was- it was the dreaded government cab voucher. The psychiatric nurse, an old white woman who looked like Rapunzel, smiled at me. It was a smile which meant "Now I've got you. All the other cab drivers have refused to come here and pick up this mentally ill patient, but you had the "luck" of being sent here and you must pick this fare up"! Really the nursing staff at the hospital knew that cab drivers hated picking up fares there because of the problems the patients created for drivers. I saw other nurses standing behind her and scrutinizing me. I stopped the car and got out to meet the man at the entrance. I told him to sit in front, but he insisted on sitting in the back. The nurses were looking at me. I was afraid they would call the Goodwill Cab Company and report me that I was not civil and cooperative with the customer. Arthur, the dispatcher, would, of course, get really angry and would not send me to pick up other fares probably for at least three hours! I really could not afford not to pick up for three hours, so, I cooperated with the fare and helped him to get in the back seat.

He got in and slammed the door of the cab so loudly I was amazed the door was still hooked on to its hinges. He was young, about twenty years old. He had a bandage around his head, probably where they had operated on his brain, but that was just a guess on my part. I also thought I saw a little blood stain on the bandage. He was fidgeting with a small transistor radio and he hit it whenever the radio announcer said something he did not like. Then a song came on, Tina Turner's "*What's love got to do with it*? He rocked from side to side to the rhythm of the song. Yet, another song *Billy Jean* by Michael Jackson came on and he rocked back and forth so vigorously I could feel the cab move from side to side! I drove down the winding slope which led out of the hill on top of which the hospital was built still incensed for being sent to Highland Psych. I told him to turn off his radio, but he refused and continued trying to search for different stations, particularly the ones that had good receptions. Then he got one and started to shake his head from side to side to the music coming from the radio. When he thought he could not hear the music well because of the problematic volume control of the old transistor radio, he would hold it to his ears rocking from side to side as before. I knew that I had picked up a problem. After about five minutes, I broke the silence between us and the following exchange transpired.

Me: We are going to 1789 82nd Avenue right?
Fare: Your Mama!
Me: What?
Fare: I'm going to your Mama!
Me: My mama?
Fare: Yeah! Man… you heard me. I said I'm going to your Mama!

I stopped for a minute. My mother was in far away Ibadan, in Nigeria, and I did not think that I could drive him in a cab to Nigeria. I was not flying an airplane!

Me: Look, I am just confirming the address that is written on this cab voucher. It says 1789 82nd Avenue, Oakland. That place is in East Oakland right? Is that where I am taking you?

Now, I had to double check all of these because the dispatcher must have a confirmation of my destination even after I picked up a fare. I must radio back to him to confirm the address in case the address on the voucher and where the fare wanted to go did not match. This was strictly standard procedure for voucher customers that Goodwill cab drivers must follow.

Me: 1789 82nd Avenue right?
Fare: No, man, take me to my Cousin's house. She's gonna make me some hamburgers!
Me: Your Cousin's house? Where is that?
Fare: In San Francisco man... What's the matter with you? When you start driving man? Are you a new cab driver or something? I said take me to my cousin's house man. You mean you don't know where that is in San Francisco?
Me: San Francisco?
Fare: Yes man, Castro Street, in San Francisco!
Me: The voucher says...
Fare: Fuck the voucher; I don't care what the voucher says!
Me: The voucher says 1789 82nd Avenue in East Oakland.
Fare: I told you, man... I ain't going to no East Oakland man. Take me to San Francisco.
Me: No, I can't do that. I will get in trouble.
Fare: Trouble? Shit! You are already in trouble! Just take me to my cousin in San Francisco.

We argued for twenty minutes about where he wanted to go. I got frustrated and parked the cab telling him to get out and that I can only take him to the address on the voucher. He got angry.

Fare: You African or something?

Me: Yes, I am African. I am a Nigerian.
Fare: African! You must be from some kind of tribe... Swahili?
Me: No, I am Yoruba.
Fare: Say something to me in Yoruhbbah man.
Me: Look, I am not in a mood for language lessons this afternoon.
Fare: Come on man... says something to me in Yoruhbbah man.
Me: *Kasan.*
Fare: What?
Me: I said *Kasan.*
Fare: What the hell does that mean man? I bet you're cursing me out, *Khason*!
Me: No, no, I said: Good afternoon.
Fare: "The hell you say... shit. I know you're cursing me out."

He grabbed the collar of my shirt from the back. I felt the pressure around my neck. Then, I heard him say "Yeah man... that's what you get for cursing me out. "Khason." What the hell is that man?" I struggled to free myself from his firm grip, but it was unyielding. I told him to get out then he said: "What the hell? I ain't getting out. Shit! You gotta take me to my cousin's house man."
"Look, I don't know where your cousin's house is, and I am not taking you anywhere anymore. Get out"! As taxi drivers, we have been trained in how to handle unruly or problematic passengers. I began rehearsing all the procedures in my head and thinking about which one I might eventually use on this fare. His eyeballs were blood shot. He rolled himself into a ball and rocked from side to side and then he spoke.

"*I ain't getting out. Take me to San Francisco*"!
"*San Francisco?*"
"*Yes. That's where I mo go now.*"
"*The voucher said...*"
"*Well, screw the voucher. I wanna go to San Francisco.*" "*Well, I am not taking you to San Francisco. Get out*"!

Suddenly, he bit me in the back of my neck and I struggled with him in order to be free from his iron grip while trying to drive the taxi with one hand. Naturally, the cab swerved from side to side, even as some pedestrians looked at us in a strange way but kept walking. No one came to my aid. Finally, I parked the cab in front of *Joe's Pizza and Restaurant*, grabbed the key because I was afraid that he might lay his hand on it, and I jumped out! He was sitting alone by himself in it singing the Negro Spiritual *Swing Low, Sweet Chariot*! Then I thought to myself… my cab was not the "Sweet Chariot" that would carry him home that afternoon. I was prepared to lose the money for the fare. All I wanted was for him to get out of my cab and walk to wherever he wanted to go.

"Come on Swahili man"!

I did not answer him.

"I'm sorry Swahili man"!

I touched the back of my neck where he had bitten me to see if he broke the skin. I did not see any blood so I was satisfied that he did not break the skin, but the spot was sore and swollen. No, I wasn't going into the cab with him still sitting in it.

Swahili man

I did not answer him.

Come on Swahili man… I' am sorry man… I didn't mean to bite you. You can talk Swahili to me all you want man. I ain't gonna bite you no more man. I am willing to learn man."

Still, I did not answer him. I walked to the entrance of Joe's Pizza and stood there fidgeting with the key to the cab. Still, he refused to get out of the cab.

Look, I told you I am not Swahili. Can't you get that into your head"?

*Alright… alright whatever you are man, it's okay man. I don't care
if you are some green man from Mars man.*

I felt offended, but I knew that all I wanted was for him to just get
out of the cab. He was holding me up from doing my driving and
making money. I could hear the obnoxious dispatcher calling me to
see if I had dropped him on 82nd Avenue and if I was ready for
another fare.

*308
Come in 308. Where are you 308?*

He was sitting in the cab. I was not about to walk to the cab and try
to answer the radio call.

*308!"
308!"
Come in 308. Hey, 308 where are you? I got a fare for you. Pick up
a fare from the Berkeley Hills. I'll give you the rest of the address
when you are near the place." I got really upset. Berkeley Hills…*

 I knew that the fare was probably going to San Francisco
International Airport. All the drivers were always wishing they
would be sent to Berkeley Hills to pick up fares. People who lived
there were consummate professionals like professors of the
University of California at Berkeley, or lawyers, medical doctors,
dentist, pharmacists, or the presidents of large companies or
corporations. They were always travelling and therefore going to
the San Francisco International Airport. That was probably a cab
ride of about forty or fifty dollars. I did not want to lose that fare. I
got even more aggravated at this point, so I went to my cab and
dragged him out even as he was yelling obscenities and scratching
my arms with his long fingernails. He got out finally and laughed at
me then he mumbled something about his cousin's house and how
he missed his cousin so much. I learned that they grew up together

in Louisiana and that their very stern and disciplined grandmother raised him and his cousin. Their grandmother made the most sumptuous jambalaya and he asked me if I had eaten jambalaya before. Then he wanted to tell me more stories about his persistently drunk grandfather who moved from Louisiana to South Carolina in search of authentic "corn whiskey." I was not in the mood to listen to any more of his stories so I walked to the other side of the cab jumped into the driver's seat and sped off leaving behind a hail of dust, smoke, and tire marks. He was visible in my rear view mirror in front of Joe's Pizza and Restaurant.

Chapter 4: (At large in California).

When I moved out of Luisah's house, in December of 1985, my wife and I were lucky to get an apartment at 1942 35th Avenue in Oakland. It was a chance meeting with an Ibo friend – Ajufoh that facilitated my move. He had told me that he was the manager of the apartment somehow and that he also lived in one of the apartments in the building. After inquiring about the monthly rent and considering whether my job as a cab driver would be enough to pay the rent, I told him that he should reserve the apartment for me. In January 1986, my family moved into the apartment. It looked like a one-bedroom apartment with an extra room, which served as the kitchen. Since the children were still young, we used the pseudo kitchen as their bedroom and placed a bunk bed there for them. The space constriction was annoying to me, but I kept two promises to my wife – we would move out of Luisah's house despite her kindness and wonderful generosity, and I would continue to work as a cab driver in order to make ends meet.

Ajufoh was a rather strange individual who lived in the apartment facing ours. He lived with his brother and was always boasting about the big connection he had with American celebrities in the movie industry. I used to look at him in awe, wondering why he did not just "connect" with these celebrities, and in that case, he could mention me. All I got from him were promises. To me, he seemed like a fighter, one who cherished any opportunity to engage in physical combat. When he got angry, he used to hit the walls with his bare fists, and when my wife and I would hear loud thuds coming from his apartment we would immediately realize that he was angry with someone or something. He was like Humpty Dumpty, a sort of overreacher whose fall was inevitable. At one time he told me he was a producer. I asked him what he produced, and he said he was a producer for the arts. I never saw him produce anything, but he used to bring home flyers, and posters of musicians, and fine artists, and at the bottom of the flyers and posters would be these words – "Produced by Ajufoh Chikamele." I used to look at the glossy flyers and posters and one day I saw one in which the artists were performing at a place called *The Western Addition* in San Francisco. I was curious that his job as a "producer" could have been a sort of Mickey Mouse operation. Just a week or so after moving into the apartment on 35th Avenue, I noticed that a woman, Phavia Kujichagulia came to visit Ajufoh. She stayed for a while with him and then left. He told me that the woman was an artist and had perfected her art as a trumpeter. He promised to introduce her to me when next she came to visit him. Meanwhile, Babatunde had put up a proposal for the Ravenswood City School District. He wanted a collaborative artistic performance for that school district so that we would be paid for our efforts. When he came to my apartment, he gave me the proposal to read. This was it:

PROPOSAL FOR CULTURAL WEEK PRESENTATION (Winter 1986)

Iroko Productions with Babatunde Kayode as Producer/Director intend to present a cultural week for the Ravenswood City School District. The cultural presentation program includes Poetry, Drama, and a Dance Performance. The poetry will be multi-faceted in nature, combining the artistic excellence of Phavia Kujichagulia – a poetess, author, and musician, Keith Archuleta – Poet, Dipo Kalejaiye- Poet/Playwright, and Babatunde Kayode- a universal artist.

The dance performance will feature Bale- Colleg, a dance company based in East Palo Alto. The play to be performed will be Their Spirits Are Free – a South African play that highlights the universal struggle of Black South Africans.

The objectives of the Cultural Presentation are as follows:

a) *To educate through the performing arts, and to show that culture is an on-going process that extends beyond the yearly Black history month which takes place every February.*

b) *To teach and present a vehicle for cultural awareness. Highlight cultural interrelationships and relevance.*

c) *To present a contextual forum for present/future adaptation or acquisition of theatrical skills.*

d) *To teach culture in a universal historical perspective via the performing arts.*

e) *To promote a heritage that will be supplemental to the school curriculum.*

The Performers:
The first performers will be Dipo and Jumoke Kalejaiye, doing poetry and music. The first poem from this team is titled Abiku – which in Yoruba belief means a child that dies, then returns to live again, that is a child doomed to an unending cycle of birth- death- and rebirth. Their second poem is titled The Daemon of the Banana Tree written by Dipo Kalejaiye, the poem was awarded the Ina Coolbirth Prize for Poetry. The daemon refers to the one the Yoruba people believe lives in a banana tree. The last poem by these performers is titled Iroko. The Iroko tree is a very powerful tree in Yoruba land which many people believe has a spirit inside it. The spirit, when provoked could come out and wreak havoc.
The next performers will be Keith Archuleta and Babatunde Kayode. They will perform Their Spirits Are Free – a South African play about Nelson Mandela and Steve Biko. Nelson Mandela the leader of the African National Congress has been jailed for 24 years. Steve Biko the leader of The Black Consciousness Movement was killed in prison. The spirit of Steve Biko comes to visit Nelson Mandela in prison. They discuss the present, past, and future of South Africa. (The *Iroko Productions Newsletter* Winter 1986).

Eventually, Phavia, and I met just before the *Ravenswood* performance. She came for a practice session in the backyard of my apartment building. Ajufoh, her producer, of course, was busy listening to her playing the trumpet in such an exquisite way. I asked her where she learned to play the trumpet so well. She only smiled and did not tell me. Although a short woman, she was beautiful in an exotic way. She was black and shining and when she smiled her teeth seemed to be the whitest in all of Oakland! She wore dreadlocks all the time, although I was sure she was not a Rastafarian like Jahman, who went around saying "Jah Rastafari" all the time. To compliment her beauty, she had the most impeccable character. She was kind, gentle, and understanding. Challenges did not seem to worry her as she faced them with her quiet charisma and strength. My wife asked me who she was and I told her that she was a jazz trumpeter who was also going to be performing at Ravenswood. I was not happy about Ajufoh's role in the whole Ravenswood affair. He was going to be "the producer" and was going to get thirty percent of whatever Ravenswood paid us. I thought he was unabashedly untalented. He would say the most inartistic things that could bring a production crashing down. I had been involved with him on a small dance performance in Berkeley, and he insisted that for a dance that involved fire, we should light a real fire on stage! I told him that we could use fire substitutes that will actually glow like fire, but would not present a fire hazard to make the Berkeley Fire Department come sounding their fire alarm. I had to drop out of the dance routine as I thought his artistic vision was a bit dangerous for me. What if a dramatic action required that someone was to kill another person on stage, would he then ask for a real murder to occur on stage?

"Well done… well done" I heard Ajufoh's raspy voice praise Phavia after she had finished a rendition of one of the tunes of Miles Davis. Phavia had dropped her surname for the African "Kujichagulia" It is a Swahili word which means self-determination. It was the second principle of the Nguzo Saba in the Kwanza (African American Holiday). The day Phavia was practicing her trumpet in our backyard; I brought out two of my djembe drums and began playing. I had been acquiring the drums for use when my wife and I would begin the Yoruba Folktale

Theatre presentations in the area. As I was playing the djembe, a man came from San Francisco to visit Ajufoh. He walked straight to the backyard where the jamming was taking place, and he unzipped his backpack and brought out a big sekere, and started playing with us. He was obviously Puerto Rican; very light skinned, and balding. He was of average height and easily given to laughter. He was always saying that we (meaning Phavia and me) should play as if we were in a "*produxion*" that is – production. He would not let us take a break insisting that we should continue to play as if we were in a "*produxion*". I became friends with Reuben because of his jolly character, and the fact that I loved to hear him say "*produxion*"! Reuben seemed to be very much in tune with the Yoruba culture as he began telling me so many things concerning Yoruba religion and culture that I wondered whether he had ever been to Yoruba land. "I am from Puerto Rico man; Yoruba culture is very popular in Puerto Rico." He said as he continued to play the sekere, breaking into a sweat instantly. He said his name was Reuben Trexidor and that he was a producer from San Francisco, and that he was looking for a group to produce.

 Finally, I told him that I wanted him to be the producer for the Amuyo African Theatre and we would be rehearsing in the backyard of our apartment a few times a week. He agreed and his fees were not as exorbitant as that of the unartistic Ajufoh. In fact, he said if we only made a little money, he would not ask for his percentage as a producer. He seemed more enthusiastic about the success of the group more than the money we could realize immediately.

After the initial visit of Reuben Trexidor to Ajufoh, my wife and I decided to begin the presentations of the Yoruba Folktales. We decided that we would take the folktales and turn them into theatrical pieces laced with music, dance, and jokes. I had the task of collecting the folktales and putting them in a certain order for performance. I structured the performance this way:

1. There would be the Ijuba (Praising the ancestors and the progenitors of Yoruba traditional performance).

2. The dramatic presentation of the folktale with music, dance, and improvisation.

3. The Finale music and dance. (We used the piece titled *Awa nlo* – We are going)

I started combing the bookstores in the area for Yoruba folktales, but I got frustrated when I could not find any! Even Adebisi Y Aromolan's bookshop in Berkeley did not have much on Yoruba folktales; I began collecting them orally, from a woman who was the mother of one of my friends in Oakland. Everyone called her "Alhaja". It was from Alhaja, that I got the following: *The Tortoise and the Dog, The Tortoise and His Wife, Simbi, The Deer-Woman of Owo, The Elephant and the Tortoise, The Dog and his Dead Mother in Heaven, Bujebuje Olunrete,* and *The Tortoise and the Hare.* I had been familiar with these folktales when I was in primary school in Nigeria, but it seemed that as time went on, they began to fade into oblivion. No one seemed to remember them or even the songs associated with them. My Yoruba friends looked at me as if I was seeking a needle in a haystack. One, whose name was Segun, said only his grandmother back in Nigeria could remember the folk tales I was seeking, and that I should wait till he got to Nigeria on vacation to ask her about them and report back to me. I only laughed and decided to follow Alhaja's instructions about the ones she had given me. She was helpful to the extent that she told me the stories and she sang the songs associated with them. I placed the nine folk tales in repertory for the group and we began rehearsing them.

Babatunde agreed to be a member of the group, and we recruited other willing African American dancers and singers for the group. Ajufoh began jostling for a place in the group, but I was at a loss as to where to put him. We already had a producer, he cannot sing or dance and he said he could not memorize anything! He would appear during our backyard rehearsals and pose as a member of the group, giving hints on what to do such as when to change drums, the use of the African gong, the position of the dancers, and their entrances and exits. Since I was the Artistic director, I tried to caution him, but he only acted as if he was the one who started the group. I used to be so impervious to his obnoxious nature, but when I could not stand it anymore, I told him he had to stay away from our rehearsals. After I had 'kicked' him out of the group so to speak, he would grab an antic looking cane chair and come out to watch the rehearsals with his huge beer mug in hand. If there was a mistake, or someone was unable to sing the Yoruba songs without an obvious African American accent, he would burst out laughing and choking on his beer. The performers would stop to look at him and wonder about his exasperating behaviour. I used to apologize on his behalf, even when one of the performers Malik Johnson asked me why "my friend" was "laughing like a hyena"; I told him that Ajufoh did not know any better. Ajufoh insisted that I could not prevent him from sitting in the backyard since it was a shared space between him and me. Phavia used to calm him down somewhat. It seemed he really liked her, but did not garner enough courage to tell her so. She was like the tempering force for his brash behaviour. Whenever he saw Phavia, he would calm down and things would go according to plan. She was just cool, like her trumpet and saxophone.

Babatunde, a member of the group was a consummate artist. He could sing, dance, memorize and improvise. I used him as one of the male lead characters in the different folk tale theatre presentations. My wife was the female lead. As the children were growing up, specifically, my daughters, Bola and Buki, we integrated them into the routine performance of the group. My son, Yinka, was annoyingly stage shy. We tried everything to make him participate in the folktale performances, but he refused to take part in even the smallest role in the performance. He did everything possible in order to avoid getting on stage. He would feign illness, or even hide under a couch or sofa. My daughters were very eager to be part of the group. My younger daughter, Buki, who had developed an ear for rhythm, became Reuben Trexidor's African gong trainer. Reuben apart from being the producer of the group would insist on playing one of the minor musical instruments such as the sekere and the African gong. I thought at the time, he was a bit overzealous. He played the gong off beat, so, one day I asked Buki if she could try a rhythm I had developed for the folktale about the tortoise and his wife. She said she would try and I was impressed that she got the rhythm correctly on the first trial. Everyone looked at her with amazement. I think Reuben got irritated that a five year old was going to teach him how to play the African gong, so he snatched the gong from Buki and began to play it, off beat of course! I directed that he should give the gong back to her and just concentrate on the sekere. He looked at me as if I gave the order because Buki was my daughter, but in reality, I made the change because she was able to get the rhythm and to stay within the beat of the djembe and the other drums. Essentially, I told Reuben that the African gong was a kind of "time keeper" and that if the time keeping was off, then the beat would be off and there would be no harmony. He looked at me as if to ask me where I went to music school, but he did not say it; he only shrugged and receded to the background chanting "*produxion*".

Soon, I began to realize that we have been rehearsing in the backyard and not getting gigs. Jumoke was the first to point that out to me, and she said that we better design flyers and posters announcing the group and our folktale theatre presentation. She volunteered to design the flyers and posters. We also agreed to contact some cultural centers and lounges where our type of entertainment would be tolerated. We knew, for example, that we could not perform at a lounge or club that was exclusively for jazz, bluegrass, or rock; we would be out of place with the clientele there. Our effort was concentrated on clubs, lounges and cultural centers of African or African American orientation. We identified a few and sent the flyers and posters there, basically announcing the group and our eagerness to perform our unique brand of folktale theatre. Reuben agreed to take a whole bunch of flyers and posters which he claimed he was going to paste all over the Bart stations in San Francisco, and some of the night clubs there. In one of my numerous trips to the city, I saw the posters of the group sometimes with part of them torn off by vandals. Some were riddled with graffiti. One day, at about noon, I was standing on Market Street in San Francisco in front of a corner grocery store. Then I saw one of our posters nailed to a lamp post. I walked up to the graffiti riddled poster of our group. One piece of writing said *"Quaint third world theatre shit"*. I burst out laughing and a blonde white woman who was pulling along her baby in a stroller was startled. She pulled her hair back, held on tightly to her purse, and with a stiff upper lip, turned the stroller in the opposite direction, pushing it as fast as possible away from me, glancing back periodically to look at me. I could see her baby, turning her neck as if to say she was supposed to be going in the direction she was fleeing from. I was really going to the Bart station so that I could get back to Oakland. When I got back home that day, I told my wife that we must do all we can to make sure that our performances were not *"Quaint third world theatre shit"*! Of course, we laughed about the whole matter, and the ever listening Ajufoh came out of his apartment to stand in his doorway looking at us and wondering what was so amusing to us.

Babatunde was getting impatient with me about the folktale theatre project. Really, he wondered why we did not get invitations from anywhere to come and perform the folktales. He accused me of complacency; then, one day, he said he had a proposition for me. When I asked him what the proposition was, he said he wanted our group to perform my play – *Danger Awake.* I was a bit reluctant about an outright stage drama presentation because I thought it would distract me from my rehearsals for the folk tale theatre, and besides, I was still a cab driver by day, at least five days a week. I did not think I could take on the rehearsals of another play. He kept trying to persuade me to stage the play. I asked him where he thought I might do it and he said The *Experimental Group Young People's Theatre* (E.G.Y.P.T). He said that Mona Gibson, the Executive Director of the theatre was his friend and that he had talked to her about me, and she was anxious to meet me. I told him I was not anxious to meet her, but Babatunde insisted. We had grown very fond of each other, and I used to call him "Dreadlock of

Oyo State". He did not have dread locks but his hair was so tangled that they looked like dreadlocks to me. He was also from Oyo state in Nigeria, particularly, the city of Ibadan. He came to see me every other week or during rehearsals for the folktales and he brought up the issue of the performance at E.G.Y.P.T. theatre. He said that the Executive Director was looking for something African, something different for the theatre-going audience of East Oakland. I gave him the script of *Danger Awake* and asked him to give it to Mona Gibson. Surprisingly, a week later, Mona called me and asked when I was going to have an audition for the play. I was disappointed; I wanted her to turn the script down so that I can concentrate on being a theatre director for the folktale project and a cab driver. I agreed to meet her the next week.

It was early February 1986 when I put up an audition notice for *Danger Awake* at EGYPT theatre. The theatre was on 5306 Foothill Boulevard Oakland. I met Mona Gibson, a petite African American woman whose husband also worked at the theatre. She was prim and had a twinkle in her eye all the time. She had a hearty kind of laughter, but was a shrewd business woman, who controlled everything about the theatre. Her husband was always hovering around her, even during his day off from the theatre, he could be heard in the carpenter's shop constructing a set piece, or backstage helping to put up flats. I had a brief meeting with Mona, who told me that the play must be staged in March, but I thought there would not be enough time for rehearsals. As usual, Babatunde urged me on and promised to help with the production in whatever capacity.

On the day of the audition, he brought in Ishmail Kaya, a Tanzanian, who was teaching in Oakland at the time. He was a tall, gaunt looking man and was so excited that an African play was going to be staged in Oakland. He tried to impress me with the fact that he and his uncle had met many important people from Nigeria when he was in Tanzania. He boasted about meeting General Olusegun Obasanjo, who was to become the first elected civilian president of Nigeria in 1999.

Others at the audition were Andrew Sali from Uganda, who had attended Sonoma State University, and the University of California at Berkeley. I used to joke around with him that we belonged to the same university alumni since I had attended the University of California at Berkeley as well. Tami France also attended the audition. She was an African American who studied acting at Contra Costa College, in San Pablo and Chabot College in Hayward. She had participated in various drama productions in the area and was a student of acting at The American Conservatory Theatre in San Francisco. Darrell S. Smith also attended the audition. He was a native of San Francisco and a percussionist. He believed in everything African and asked everyone to call him "Ibo", and he had changed his name to a Yoruba, one (Akinlana Sangotosin) Two Nigerians, Kareem Adetokunbo, and Femi Sonuga also attended the audition. Kareem was born in Kensington, London. His parents brought him to the United States when he was only two years old and had lived there ever since. Femi Sonuga was an aspiring filmmaker whose brother Gbenga Sonuga, was an actor and the Director of the Lagos State Council for Arts and Culture in Nigeria. He used to boast that he was born into a theatre arts family. I made my cast selection this way:

DANGER –   Ishmail Kaya
LT. ADE GOMA   (Danger's friend) - Babatunde Kayode
DR. SIJU MALA   -   (An Army Captain) - Andrew Sali
BINTU (Goma's wife) Tami France
STORYTELLER: Phavia Kujichagulia
IFA PRIEST: Dipo Kalejaiye
SOLDIERS   Femi Sonuga and Adetokunbo Amole
DRUMMER"   Darrell Smith (Akinlana
Sangotosin)
TRUMPETER   Phavia Kujichagulia.

Mona Gibson had insisted that I should direct the play. That reminded me of what Nora

Vaughn did to me at the Black Repertory Theatre, when she insisted that I direct *The Graduate Palava*. At the production meeting I had with Mona, her husband, and other members of the theatre administration, I pleaded with Mona to support my effort in finding a director for the play, but she said she knew no one who could take on the job because it was an African play, and I certainly could not find anyone either. Finally, I made up my mind again, to direct the play. One disappointing thing to me was the fact that the African American actor I had cast as the Ifa Priest, Travis Smith, dropped out of the impending production three weeks before the show. Travis had complained that he would never be able to speak in incantations the way the Ifa Priest spoke in the play. He also found the Yoruba proverbs and philosophical allusions intimidating. I had to play the role of the Ifa Priest!

The rehearsals went well for the most part, and Mona was always around in the evenings to watch its progress. She would stand outside the theatre for a while, chain-smoking and chatting with her doting husband, and as soon as she enters the theatre to watch our rehearsals, her husband would follow her into the theatre.

It was the end of February 1986, the publicity for the play was not yet out, and so, I complained to Mona about it. I told her that we should not have to perform for an empty house. Then she took a pencil and asked me to give her a summary of the play. I told her that the action of the play took place in Nigeria, during the infamous Lagos bar beach public executions of armed robbers. I told her that an armed robber whose name was "Danger" had been caught by the authorities and was executed in a similar fashion. The leader of the firing squad was Lieutenant Ade Goma and that when the armed robber died; he was refused entry into heaven and hell. So he came back to earth to torment Goma. She thought the story was brilliant and did not finish hearing the rest of it when she ordered that the publicity for the play should go out to all the major newspapers in the area.

Meanwhile, my wife was getting impatient with me. She thought I should put in more hours at the cab company working, perhaps seven days a week. I told her that directing the play and also playing the role of the Ifa Priest in it was too cumbersome and I was not going to drive a cab seven days a week as that would make the drama production impossible. She thought I was being impractical and that the theatre was really paying me nothing, and that it was from being a taxi driver that I could make a living to support the family. I had to convince her that I had not quit my job as a cab driver, but the production was in about three weeks and it had to be successful. She agreed with me reluctantly. She was also looking for a job to help support the family. She had applied to many establishments, but with no success, and was getting restless.

One day, as I was driving my cab marked "308" on East 14th Street in Oakland, the dispatcher sent me a radio message to pick up a fare in North Oakland. I proceeded to the address and when I got there I parked outside the white and brown house and waited for the person to come out. I was surprised to see a rather short, very dark skinned African American woman come out dressed like one of the Osun worshippers of Ile Orunmila Oshun! She had an infectious smile and a dimple on her right cheek. Her makeup was moderate, but it seemed that her red lipstick was overdone. She had sleepy bedroom eyes, which seemed mysterious to me. For reasons known to her, she was always dabbing her eyes with a large white handkerchief. I thought there was something African in her bold facial structure. She wore a gorgeous ankle length white lace gown with a white headgear to match and many rows of bracelets and necklaces. Two of the necklaces were made of very thick red, yellow, and green beads; they were *Mardi Gras* necklaces, it made her look like a voodoo priestess. "Good morning," she said as she entered the cab and closed the door. "Good morning" I replied, glancing at her in the rear view mirror. She smiled when she caught me glancing at her in the mirror. Her teeth were white except one that the dentist had capped with gold fillings. I could smell her perfume which was going to saturate the inside of the cab, long after I had dropped her in downtown Oakland. "My name is T. J. Robinson" she spoke in a very refined manner and with a voice which was very musical. "I am Dipo Kalejaiye. I live in Oakland," I answered. Then she told me that she was originally from Louisiana and that she owned a restaurant in downtown Oakland called *The Ginger Bread House.* She said that the restaurant was situated in the Jack London Square area. We continued talking and I told her that I was a Yoruba from Nigeria, and that I was even directing a play for E.G.Y.P.T theatre and that if her busy schedule could permit, she should come and watch it. Then I told her that my wife had just arrived from Nigeria and that she was looking for a job. She told me to tell her to come for an interview the next day. I was surprised to hear that when she had not even filled out an application!

When I got home, I told my wife about my encounter with T.J. Robinson, the restaurant owner. That very week, my wife began working as a hostess at *The Gingerbread House.* It turned out that the most famous menu item in the restaurant was a dish known as Jambalaya! That automatically reminded me of Luisah's book- *Jambalaya,* and the Louisiana Cajun/creole roots of T.J. Robinson.

When my wife started working at Gingerbread House, a second income made things a little better for us as a family. She was still looking at me with suspicion because of my energetic involvement in various theatrical activities. She argued that they were not bringing in money and that I ought to concentrate on more menial jobs, maybe working another job apart from driving a taxi. The cab driving was not yielding much, and that was another sore point for her. Things got serious when I told her that I was directing my play in E.G.Y.P.T theatre in Oakland. Immediately, she asked me how much they were going to pay me. I could not mention a dollar amount because whatever Mona was going to pay me was going to be commensurate with how much they realized from the box office sales of tickets. I had become a bit disillusioned as I thought the publicity for the play was not going well. If people did not know about the play, they cannot come to see it and there would be no ticket sales. An argument ensued between my wife and I because she saw me as doing something not very practical – trying to realize money from dramatic productions. She asked me to tell her how much I thought I would realize to take care of two daughters and a son. Inside me, I was afraid she had a point. She had always been very pragmatic and intelligent. Her uncanny ability to be so right was always shocking to me. One day, as I was perusing the local newspapers I saw the following in the *Oakland Tribune*:

Actors from Nigeria, Tanzania, and Uganda, are taking part in the production of Danger Awake. A symbolic comedy-drama about contemporary African social issues at EGYPT theatre in Oakland. It is written and directed by Nigerian born Dipo Kalejaiye who has worked with Berkeley's Black Repertory theatre. Fridays, Saturdays, and Sundays at 4.p.m through April 27 at 5306 Foothill Boulevard Oakland. 436-4877.

I had picked up the paper during my daily run as a cab driver. So when I got home that evening I walked in with a swagger and threw the newspaper on my wife's lap where she sat on the living room armchair, and I told her that the publicity for my play was finally out and that I wanted her to see it. Characteristically, she did not touch the newspaper, but instead turned up the television, and concentrated on what she was watching. "I said the publicity of the play is finally out," I said to her in an excited manner, but she replied by saying "so what do you want me to do about it? By the way, how much did you make from driving a cab today?" I was incensed. She had not even opened the paper to the page where the publicity for the play was and on top of that, she was asking me how much I made driving the cab that day. Finally, she reluctantly lifted the newspaper up and looked at the advertisement about the play; then she threw the newspaper on the floor carelessly and resumed watching her television program. I still wanted to impress her that my semi-professional incursion into the San Francisco bay area theatre circuit may pay off eventually. So, I whipped out *The East Bay Express* from the back pocket of my jeans. I had neatly folded page twenty-seven of the paper and kept it there. "Here, take a look at another advert about the play in the *East Bay Express,*" I said, trying to win her over to my side somehow. The paper had written their advertisement for the play this way:

Egypt Theatre and Iroko Productions present Amuyo African Theatre in Danger Awake, written and directed by Dipo Kalejaiye at 8.p.m Fridays and Saturdays, 4.p.m Sundays at 5306 Foothill Blvd. Oakland 436-4877

This time, she refused to touch the newspaper, but she got up and went into the kitchen, leaving me standing in the middle of the living room bewildered. I garnered enough courage to go and give the advertisements to the flamboyant Ajufoh whom I thought would have a field day going around to his many friends to show them the newspaper clippings. I also told him to please make sure that he invited as many of his friends as possible, and that admission was not free, except for him for whom I knew I could arrange a complimentary ticket.

The rehearsals for the play were going well, but we had challenges with the procurement of costumes. Finally, I contacted Solomon Rasheed, Yemisi Laditan, Remi Omodele, Titi Bankole, and an African American who only gave his name as "Jheri", for help with the costumes. Everything was going well until Jheri was to do the makeup for Ishmail Kaya who played the lead role. I realized that Ishmail was always trying to avoid Jheri. I thought that was odd, as that was the person who would do his makeup. Ishmail had to wear a sort of cape and a mask to simulate the effect of his being a ghost. There was always riotous laughter whenever Jheri would sit him down in the costume room to apply the makeup and Ishmail, of course, would bolt away at the feel of Jheri's fingers on his face, knocking over everything and even Mona's coffee pot that was brewing by the entrance into the theatre. Jheri, of course, would be pursuing him all over the theatre asking him to come back and finish his make up and not waste his time. The rehearsals would come to a halt with everyone laughing at the show Ishmail and Jheri presented. Really, their game of running around the building and playing hide and seek looked like a classic cat and mouse game. So, one day I asked Ishmail what the problem was and he complained that he thought Jheri wanted to "marry him". I laughed and told him that such a thing was impossible, it was then that he told me that he thought Jheri was making him "too effeminate" for a courageous Nigerian armed robber of the 1970s. Then, Ishmail pulled me aside and said that he thought Jheri was gay and that he did not like how he was caressing his face as if he was his "wife". I pleaded with Ishmail that he should please take it all in strides and that the production was in two weeks and we had to all concentrate and cooperate in order to have a successful production. Their tryst seemed to hamper the rehearsals for about a few days, so I concentrated on rehearsing the chorus in the original songs I had composed for the play such as "*Story oh! My Story, The Order to Ponder*" and "*The Song of the Sufferer*". As I would be rehearsing these songs with the chorus and with the beautiful trumpet backing of Phavia, Ishmail and Jheri would stop their bickering and miraculously walk back into the theatre to listen to the voice of the chorus. But as soon as I was done with that bit, they would go at it again, with Ishmail running away from Jheri and the latter in hot pursuit out of the theatre onto Foothill Boulevard! It crossed my mind to write a one act play just about this hilarious phenomenon. I could not believe that I was actually able to give direction to Ishmail after all since he spent so much time "dodging" Jheri. Ishmail was very smart and intelligent. I thought he knew that. He would walk into the rehearsal without a script in hand, rendering his lines and that of others effortlessly. My feeling was that perhaps being a school teacher taught him discipline and commitment. His only drawback was that he was not a modest man.

At rehearsals, Andrew Sali, who played the Army Captain was the exact opposite of Ishmail. He was calm and accepted direction very easily. Phavia was wonderful. She was a juxtaposition of talent and energy. I cast her in the double role of Trumpeter and Storyteller. She was the one who actually began the play with the song "*Story Oh! My Story*." I had no problems with her; in fact, she doubled as an assistant to me during the rehearsal process. The soldiers, Femi and Kareem were impressive in their marching routine, and they blended well with the song "*Monkey Dey Chop Banana*".

Finally, during the last week before the opening night, many newspapers carried the advertisement about the play. Even, *The San Francisco Chronicle* mentioned it in their Sunday edition.

The week before the opening night was when my wife began to work at the Gingerbread House. She was excited to get out of the house after she had been seeking a job for a while. She came back home that day to tell me many stories about the restaurant. She said it was a quite cozy place with a real fireplace, and that the atmosphere was very warm and friendly. She also said that the guests gave her a lot of tips. The hostesses wore a white and a brown pinafore with a white gown beneath it. They were supposed to sing and dance for their guests. I asked her if she was able to sing and dance for the guests that week, but she said she could not, but that another hostess whose name was Noel taught her some of the songs they had to sing for the guests. She said that one of the main items on the menu list was a dish called Jambalaya, which was a hodgepodge of different ingredients like meat, sausage, shrimp, liver, and okra with spices that replicated Cajun/Creole cooking of Louisiana. She also told me about the famous cornbread that was always dripping with butter, and the chocolate chip cookie they served with ice cream that was usually dripping with warm chocolate or caramel. Instantly, I thought I had to visit the place, but my wife said that she would have to make a reservation for us as a family as the place was always crawling with dinner guests and that it was a hot spot for African American movie stars who were visiting the San Francisco Bay area. Apparently, the owner had a policy of asking any worker there to bring the whole family for a once in a lifetime dinner experience and they would eat free. It was later that my wife and I took advantage of that opportunity and we took the whole family of five down there. The girls had a ball and they kept making fun of the jambalaya dish, calling it "*jambalese*."

It was about three weeks after my wife started working at the Gingerbread house that she came home with an autographed copy of the black and white picture of an African American movie actor who had come to the restaurant to eat with other movie actors. At first, I did not believe her, but when she pulled out the autographed photograph of Louis Gossett Jr. I immediately saw that she had actually met him at the restaurant. The autograph said: **"To Jumoke Peace Always, From Louis Gossett Jr".** I told her that he was an important African American actor who played the endearing role of "Fiddler" in the ABC miniseries adaptation of Alex Haley's novel, *Roots,* in 1977. I thought perhaps Jumoke should have mentioned to Louis Gossett that I was doing a play at EGYPT theatre and perhaps his busy schedule permitting, he could drop by to see it. However, I asked her if she sang and danced for Louis Gossett, she answered angrily by saying "What kind of question is that? It was part of my job to sing and dance for guests at the restaurant" Then a certain voice in me said perhaps Louis Gossett will seduce my wife, but I discarded the thought as naïve and baseless. I ended up joking with her that she would have to sing and dance for me too, since I was a stage actor at least! So, I began chasing her around the living room and into the bedroom. While we were there, I could hear my daughters from the living room saying "Mummy and Daddy have started again." The girls were used to our jovial and playful manner and the fact that we laughed a lot whenever we were together, swapping jokes, and laughing into the wee hours of the morning. She bolted away from the bedroom and came back to meet the girls, Bola and Buki, insisting that they must bring out their homework for her to see.

Just before the opening of the play, a San Francisco Bay area newspaper, - *The Sun Reporter* carried an elaborate write up about the play in their Lifestyles Section. The write up was complete with the pictures of the cast members and me, and another picture of me by itself on a separate page. This was the write-up.

E.G.Y.P.T PRESENTS AFRIKAN THEATRE
The Experimental Group Young People's Theatre (E.G.Y.P.T.) in Oakland, in association with Iroko Productions, present Amuyo African Theatre Company in a play entitled Danger Awake. Amuyo African Theatre Company is a group of highly talented African and African American actors and actresses, who are dedicated to the exposure, advancement, and celebration of African theatre. In the bay area or in the United States at large, there exists a vast cultural vacuum to be filled via African theatre productions. The Amuyo African Theatre was formed in 1985 to bring authentic African plays to theatre conscious Bay area residents. It is a project designed to capture and highlight the depth, complexity, peculiar staging techniques, and the infectious nature of the African theatre. It is on the strength of these guises that Danger Awake is being staged. Danger Awake is a musical drama which utilizes the satirical concept to examine contemporary social issues in modern African society; Issues such as armed robbery and the concept of contemporary African political structure are explored in relation to the execution of justice. The examination of the absurdist inherent in the political and social process becomes an inevitable precipitation of this hilarious dramatic comedy.
Danger Awake opens on March 21st, 1986 at Experimental Group Young People's Theatre (E.G.Y.P.Y.) which is located at 5306 Foothill Boulevard. Oakland, California. Danger Awake is scheduled to run for six weeks. Fridays, and Saturdays at 8.p.m., And Sundays at 4 p.m. For ticket information, call (415) 436 0487

It was the opening night at EGYPT. My heart was pounding. I had called off driving a taxi at least for that day to make sure that everything went well. That irked my wife, Jumoke, a wonderful woman of great intellect, beauty, charisma, and perseverance, who could not be persuaded that another of my adventure into a theatrical enterprise was worth it. To her, I was this pseudo-bohemian who was on the brink of blooming into a full-fledged proper bohemian. She accused me of "living on the edge." She thought I was only using my day job as a cab driver as a ruse for what I was really interested in doing – being involved in theatre. She once argued that how many Nigerian actors have I observed in Hollywood and that the white Americans were not going to give too many African Americans "a break" into the movie industry, how much more an African immigrant with a Yoruba accent like me. She asked me if I had ever heard of something called "racial discrimination". She reminded me that Ronald Reagan was President of the United States and that the " conservative agenda" was on, even immigration, which partly concerned us at the time, was not free from Reagan's probing eyes. She thought, perhaps, I was living in some form of abandoned illusion that could only engender financial disaster. I used to shudder at her ability to be decisive, correct and brilliant. Sometimes, with her, I felt like a pupil in front of a schoolteacher. I kind of liked that a lot, because I thought, as the Americans felt, that "one's wife must be the better half"! I could not imagine marrying anyone I was "better" than, that would have been a recipe for disaster. The African Americans while speaking in some form of slang would say that something "is deep." I feel like my wife is really "deep". She is like a fully loaded oil barrel compared to an empty one that makes so much noise as it rolls down the hill unabated.

Concerning the day I had taken off at the Goodwill Cab Company, she felt that it was a whole day's income I had thrown away. Ignoring her as she fussed with the children about doing some household chores, I sneaked out of the house to go to the theatre. I had to make sure that the costumes, set, lighting and props were all in order. Particularly, I wanted to make sure that the actors were prompt. The ever professional Phavia was the first to arrive with her twin daughters and her trumpet. Ishmail came next entering the theatre with a swagger. In my mind, I was saying "Yes, you can walk in here with a swagger all you want, but you better not forget any lines." The universal artist, Babatunde, came next munching on a Macdonald's Fish fillet sandwich and sipping a strawberry shake with a straw from a Styrofoam cup. Andrew Sali and the other Nigerian actors Femi and Kareem came next, and the others followed soon after. It was when I saw that the cast had arrived on schedule that the tension I kept feeling at the back of my neck eased up a little. I scrambled into the green room to look at Jheri doing his make up on Ishmail who kept squirming in anger. I told Ishmail to calm down as the opening night was not the night to be uncooperative with Jheri. Ishmail looked at me as if to say "You are crazy, you don't really know how I feel about this guy." Jheri, on the other hand, was wringing his hands in consummate delight, relishing the fact that he got Ishmail where he wanted him- right beneath his nose and accepting the makeup he was applying whether he liked it or not. I took one look at the makeup he applied and told him that it was too overdone and that it made Ishmail look like *Count Dracula*. I told him that I did not want to create a Dracula image in an African play that was a socio-political satire. Jheri listened to me and began to remove some of the outlandish makeup. Ishmail breathed a sigh of relief and looked at me as some kind of "messiah" who had saved him from Jheri. Mona's husband, Todd, came into the Green Room to say "ten minutes to curtain." In a very business-like manner and he disappeared. I ran to the lobby of the theatre to see how many audience members had arrived. There must have been about fifteen or twenty. They were murmuring and munching on the cookies Mona had placed on a table immediately one entered the theatre. There were coffee, tea, and some soft drinks on the table as well. I ran backstage to make sure that the actors were in their places, even as I heard Todd's bass voice calling them to be in their places. The play began in earnest and I was pleased with the opening song *"Story oh! My story"*- a song my older daughter, Bola, loved so much she asked me which Nigerian musician composed the song. When I told her that it was my original composition, she was surprised and said she never knew that I could compose a song. I thought the performance went well, judging from the noise and the applause from the auditorium during the show. After the performance, a few people asked to see the playwright. To my surprise, some of the members of the audience lined up in front of me with their program notes in hand. It was Todd who told me that it was customary for audience members to have their program notes autographed if the playwright was in the audience and they liked the show. I reluctantly signed at least ten program notes feeling a bit flattered.

The week of the opening of the performance of *Danger Awake* the Nigerian Association of the United States invited me to the twenty-sixth-anniversary celebration of the Nigerian Independence. There were big posters advertising the event. One of the posters reads this way:

CELEBRATE NIGERIA'S TWENTY-
SIXTH YEAR
INDEPENDENCE ANNIVERSARY
1960-1986 JOIN US.

The event was to take place in Albany, a small town near Berkeley. The organizers were Nigerians I had known from when I was an undergraduate. They sent me a program of events and pleaded with me to please, in their words, "come and grace the occasion." I asked them if that was all they wanted. But their secretary, Dr. Austin Ahanotu, said he had heard a lot about me and that they said I was a poet and a playwright, and he would like me to come and read some of my poems at the event. I showed their invitation to my wife, and in her usual manner, she seemed disinterested in the affair, when she found out that it was going to be on Saturday when I was supposed to be making money as a cab driver. The program itself was structured in this manner:

SLIDE SHOW OF NIGERIA'S ARTS AND CULTURE by Iheanyi
Nwogu
VARIETY SHOW
BRAKE DANCING

AFRICAN POEMS by Dipo Kalejaiye
TRADITIONAL ROOTS OF ROLLER SKATING by James
Esoimeme
SYMPOSIUM: NIGERIA A NEW PERSPECTIVE.
PANEL: Dr. John Ogbu, Dr. Cheryl Ajirotutu, Dr. Aguibou
Yansane, Dr. Austin Ahanotu.
AFRICAN FASHION SHOW: By Adunni Agbabiaka
NIGERIAN CULTURAL DANCES by A. Ezenwama
I accepted the invitation and read my poems at the event.

It was now 1987 and I was still a cab driver to keep body, soul, and family together, and my wife was still working at Gingerbread House, then I saw an advert about The California
Arts Council in a local newspaper. The Council asked for artists to apply for a fellowship. This was publicized as a News Release. Unfortunately, the art I was interested in was dramatic art, and that was not on their list that year. So, I told my wife that it was time to jump start our folktale theatre project. About some weeks later, Reuben appeared at my door, excited and saying *"produxion"*. I asked him what he was so excited about, but he just kept saying *"produxion"*. I looked at his hands and he was clutching many yellow flyers. I asked him to come in and sit down. He sat down and showed me one of the flyers. This was the flyer:
RUBEN TREXIDOR PRODUCTION
 PRESENTS:
AMUYO AFRICAN THEATRE
FOLKTALE THEATRE FROM NIGERIA
A BOLD, AUTHENTIC PERFORMANCE OF YORUBA
FOLKTALES
WITH MUSIC, DANCE, AND DRAMA
Saturday, June 27, 1987.
8. P.M.
Western Addition Cultural Centre
762 Fulton Street, San Francisco
For Information 564-3931

Tickets $6:00.

My wife and I looked at Ruben with astonishment. He had quietly gone to do all the necessary work involved in getting us a gig at the San Francisco Western Addition Cultural Centre! It was as if I was looking for a miracle. Ruben even used his own money to print the flyers. My wife grabbed the flyer and looked at it. I knew that she was a fastidious woman and it would take more of a genius to impress her. She told him that she liked it and that she did not know that he had been working behind the scene to get us a gig. Momentarily, I felt vindicated. Here was a theatrical project Jumoke supported and in which she was willing to participate. Ruben grinned satisfactorily, and said we should be ready for the *"produxion"*. As usual, he could not pronounce the "c" in the word – production. We reviewed the financial arrangement between the cultural center and Amuyo African Theatre, and we agreed that it was suitable. He asked me to produce a write up that the audience could pick up at the lobby table of the cultural center as soon as they entered for the performance. Luckily, I had been working on such a write-up. Here it is:

THE AMUYO AFRICAN THEATRE
WEST AFRICAN FOLKTALE THEATRE PROJECT.
The Amuyo African Theatre is dedicated to the performance of authentic Yoruba Folktale
Theatre. The performance is based solely on the famous folk tale of the Yoruba people of Nigeria, West Africa. The stories are performed as dramas within an infectious medium of music, dance, poetry, and drama. The presentation is often divided into three sections.
The first section consists of the Ijuba that is the praise, or the invocation. It is the traditional Yoruba call for the presence and blessings of the ancestors and the gods. It is also an Ifa dance and song sequence, a dramatic invocation of the god of divination, Orunmila, to be present at the performance and make it divine.

Immediately after this song and dance routine, a second song is introduced. We call this the "call song" inviting the audience to become performers and not merely spectators. The song is titled "onile" which means "all and sundry", that is, everyone should join in the entertainment.

The second section consists of the folktales. Here, the tales are brought to fruition through a calculated dramatic enactment. Improvisation plays a key role in the realization of the dramatic effect. The original songs and sketches of Dipo Kalejaiye are added to provide variety and originality. Some of the stories in this section are: The Tortoise and the Dog, The Tortoise and the Hare, The Tortoise and his wife, Yannibo, The Tortoise and Princess Bujebuje, Olurombi, Simbi and the Handsome Stranger, The Dog and his dead Mother in Heaven, and The Hunter and the Deer Woman of Owo.

The third section consists of ending songs and dances which serve as a finale for the show. The objective of the Folktale Theatre is to turn the ordinary story telling situation into a bold Theatre piece through the well practiced improvisational method of the actors. There is a solid artistic freedom for the performers to change or shorten a piece for dramatic effect. The moral endings of the tales are sometimes subordinate to the dramatic effect.

The Folktale Theatre has been successfully presented at Stanford University in Palo Alto, California, and The Oakland Ensemble Theatre in Oakland, California.

DIPO KALEJAIYE
ARTISTIC DIRECTOR.

As usual, Ruben was excited and he took a copy of this write up with him, promising to make copies of it with his own money again, for the cultural center on the day of our performance. He left my house still chanting *"produxion"* and grinning satisfactorily as before.

On the day of the performance at the Western Addition Cultural Centre, I was surprised to see people standing outside of the center before we even got there. I was happy; that was at least one place I could remember where enthusiasm for our impending performance reached a satisfactory level. By my calculation, the spectators must have been standing at the door at least an hour and a half before we got there. Customarily, the center, only opened an hour before any show, so I felt that at least we should get a good crowd for our performance that day. As soon as my car pulled up to a metered parking space in front of the center, I jumped out to begin to bring out our drums. Babatunde was with me and gave me a helping hand. My wife shepherded the girls, Bola, and Buki, away from the hurrying Fulton Street traffic, into the safety of the center. My son, Yinka, was of course not going to participate in the performance, but he came along anyway.

"Oh! Nice, where is this drum from?" A brunette white woman with very thick lenses for eyeglasses inquired as she turned away from the poster of the group she was reading slapped on the main door of the theatre. "From Nigeria" I answered, afraid that if I allowed her to engage me in any sort of conversation she would deplete the time allotted to us for setting up for the show. "Oh honey, come and see the drums from Nigeria" she beckoned to her husband who stood with a cluster of people who were already clutching their tickets like prized possessions. I looked at my wife with satisfaction. This, hopefully, was going to be a show that would yield us some financial gain. "So, what is the name of the drum" the husband asked. "A talking drum" I replied. "Can I touch it?" The husband asked, but I told him that not before the show, but after the show, there would be ample time for him to feel the drum and even try his hands on it if he wanted. More people arrived and they were trying to huddle close to the door of the center in order to avoid the busy sidewalk.

The show began in earnest and we were able to perform about six out of the eleven or so pieces we had in repertory. After the show, a heavily bearded reporter for *The San Francisco Chronicle* wanted to interview my wife and I. He said he loved my wife's dancing and the part where the Tortoise ate his wife's porridge and he got pregnant instead of his wife! He interviewed us and promised to do a write up on our group which would appear in the paper's Thursday issue. That gig earned the group about $1600 dollars, but when we subtracted the cost of the production and Ruben's cut as "the producer" my wife and I were able to take home about $800 dollars. My wife thought that was impressive for a one night gig in San Francisco. I felt good that at least the theatrical engagement was not a failure. Babatunde kept telling me that we needed to follow up our success in San Francisco with other performances. My wife eyed him with caution thinking that he was trying to push me more into a kind of starving artist syndrome. She felt that one successful gig did not guarantee the success of all other gigs, and I should not let Babatunde influence me too much in running around and looking for gigs. Ordinarily, she eyed him with suspicion when she asked him what he did for a living and he replied that he was a "film maker"! Jumoke thought that meant he had no job! At any rate, he got us a gig at a place called *The La Pena Cultural Centre* located on Shattuck Avenue in Berkeley. The place was a Latin American hodgepodge of politics, ideas, radicalism, feminism, meeting place, dance floor, artistic classes, bar, lounge, stage, and piping hot Latin American cuisine. Ordinarily, I would visit a place for our gigs at least a week before the gig. So I went there to look around a week before our performance there. I was pleased to see the cultural ambiance of the place and the proud Latin American culture on display there. I convinced myself that what we would be doing a week later could not be too far from the cultural melting pot that was the La Pena Cultural Centre. Of course, our culture was Yoruba, and Nigerian, it should be appreciated by the clientele of the center. The La Pena Cultural Centre was established as a political entity in 1975 in response to the dictatorship of the Chilean dictator- Augusto Pinochet. It became the hub of the community. Part of their philosophy stated that they were committed to peace, social justice, the struggle against racism, sexism, compassion for all, and respect for the earth's resources. Our performance at La Pena Cultural

Centre took place on June 21, 1987. My wife designed the flyers for the performance. The flyer carried the following information:

AMUYO AFRICAN THEATRE
PRESENTS:
FOLKTALE THEATRE FROM NIGERIA.
A bold and authentic performance of Yoruba folktales, complete with music, dance, and poetry.
DATE: FRIDAY, October 30, 1987
PLACE: LA PENA CULTURAL CENTRE 3105 Shattuck Avenue, Berkeley.
TIME: 7:30p.m
Gate: $5.
Come and Crown Father's Day with this unique entertainment.
Come one come all.

It was quite a sight watching her make the flyer for something she so much railed against. She even drew a picture of an African woman fetching water from a river and putting it into a clay pot. I thought that was brilliant since my conception of the word "Amuyo" was a shortened form of a river "Alamuyo" which was in Ibadan, Nigeria, where I grew up. I used to go to this Alamuyo River to fetch water for my mother. Alamuyo in Yoruba really means "what one drinks and becomes satisfied". For this performance, my two daughters were also part of the cast and my son, as usual, sat in the audience watching us on stage. When the performance was going on, occasionally I heard him say "Mummy" when my wife appeared on stage as the wife of the Tortoise in the folktale- *The Tortoise and His Wife*, which triggered a round of laughter from the audience. The performance at La Pena did not yield as much as that of the Western Addition Cultural Centre in San Francisco. My wife and I did not talk much about it, but we both felt that the group's performance had been outstanding and that it looked as if we were getting better in our act.

It was January 1988, and the La Pena Cultural Centre telephoned me to ask if Amuyo African Theatre would like to come back to perform at the center. My wife had gone to Gingerbread House when I received the call. When she got home, I told her about the phone call from La Pena. She placed her bag down, offered me some of the gingerbread cookies she was eating, and asked me what I want to do about the invitation. I told her that we would have to accept it and go into rehearsals right away. She agreed. I had misplaced the phone numbers of some of the members of the group, so I had to rummage in my portfolio, looking for them. I found three phone numbers, Darrell's, Isonke Rukiya's, and that of Tami France. Isonke Rukiya was a light skin African American woman who had told me point blank that she was jealous of us Africans in that we had a culture, and we were always walking around with "pride and dignity" She said she had to shelve her "slave name" for the more African sounding "Isonke Rukiya". She wanted to visit Africa one day and was always happy when any discussion about Africa took place. In order not to make her envious, I used to try to muster a bit of Americanisms around her, but that would only backfire as she would say something like "Stop being patronizing Dipo, you are a real African man, why don't you want to use your fingers to eat your food?" I would laugh, give up my play acting, and immediately fall into being myself. But that would not stop her from being jealous of my wife and me. She used to ask me to teach her Fela's songs saying that his music sounded like jazz to her. I phoned the three members of the group and they agreed to participate in the upcoming La Pena performance. In December of 1987, the La Pena Cultural Centre Calendar for January 1988 came out, and in that calendar, our performance was listed this way.

LA PENA CULTURAL CENTRE CALENDER JANUARY 1988.
Amuyo Theatre Presents Folktale Theatre. A dramatic re-enactment of Nigerian folktales with music, dance, and poetry. Performed by Jumoke and Dipo Kalejaiye, and the Amuyo Theatre Ensemble. January 10, 1988. 7 p.m. $5.

The performance at La Pena was only three months to the delivery of my second son Abayomi. I persuaded my wife not to participate in it, but she insisted on participating saying that she was fine and I was only being a worrywart. On the night of the performance, when we arrived at the center, Chilean music, and particularly Salsa, music was playing very loudly. The center was full of people from Chile, Brazil, Nicaragua, Peru, The Andes, and Mexico. There were also white Americans in the center. They were talking, laughing, drinking beer, and consuming mounds of Chilean cuisine.

Some of the menu items were Arollado de Chancho - chunks of pork wrapped in pork fat smothered in red ají (Chili). Bistec a lo Pobre - Beefsteak, French fries, fried onions, topped with a couple of fried eggs. Carbondale - meat soup with finely diced beef and all kinds of vegetables such as potatoes, onions, carrots, broccoli, green pepper, and parsley. Everything smelled good, and there were spontaneous Salsa dancers on the dance floor directly opposite the entrance to the center. The members of the group entered with our musical instruments and costumes, with my two daughters bringing up the rear and arguing about who gets more of the candy I had bought for them earlier. No one seemed to care about us. As long as they were in that center, they were all just carried away by the euphoria of the infectious music, endless chatter, and of course, good food. One stocky man, with a very bushy and dark mustache, was dressed in a white top and white pair of pants to match. His cowboy boots got up to his knees, momentarily; I wondered if he had a horse in a stable outside! His dressing reminded me of the legendary Pancho Villa. He wore a huge cowboy hat made of straw and as soon as I entered, he took off his hat in greeting to me, smiled, and said something to me in Spanish I did not understand. The only word I caught in his speech was "*Amigo*" which I knew meant "friend".

I shrugged and went straight up to the dance floor where we were supposed to perform. But the Salsa dancers had invaded the place before we arrived and I asked my wife if she thought we could use our Yoruba folk tales to beat the infectious Salsa music I was hearing. She only smiled and said that as soon as we begin our show, the Salsa should die down and everyone would come and watch us. I shook my head and said that I believed that the show that night might be an uphill task as our clientele seemed to be so steeped in Latin American culture to care about our own African culture. I had a ball trying to convince the dancers that we had a show there that Sunday. As soon as I broke off one couple of dancers, two more couples climbed the stage! Babatunde stood in the back near the entrance, covered his mouth with his hands and was laughing. I was incensed. I was not supposed to be the only one to reign in these runaway dancers, why was he standing in the back and laughing at my frustration? I beckoned to him to please come and join me.in the exercise. My wife, who was of course six months pregnant sat on the edge of the stage away from the dancers and my daughters sat beside her. Luckily, I got the two couples off the stage managing to say "*Vamoose por favour*" which I thought meant "leave please" in Spanish, but I was not sure. Miraculously, the two couples left the stage, even as one of them shook hands with me, for what reason I did not know. The stage was now clear, but the Salsa music was still playing.

More people came into the center, and I thought if all these people paid five dollars each to come and see our show that Sunday evening, then we were in luck. Disappointedly, about six more couples and other dancers climbed onto the stage! I felt helpless; Babatunde finally came up to me as he saw that the situation was out of hand. We marched to the Manager, who was sitting by the grill in the kitchen sipping a Mexican beer, and smoking profusely. He was a short, balding man with two front gold teeth. "*Amigo, no problemo,*" (friend, no problem), he said in Spanish to my complaint that we were supposed to perform on the stage, and we were having difficulty clearing it because of the Salsa dancers. He got up and went back into the main section of the center with us. Then, he climbed up to the raised stage and spoke in Spanish to the dancers asking them to leave the stage. They seemed disappointed that he of all people would come there to break up their fun. But he seemed adamant as he stood there slapping his right thigh with his palm and speaking in Spanish. Finally, I heard the volume of the Salsa music go down and the pugnacious dancers left the stage.

Before the performance began, I kept wondering how many people out of the big crowd in the center, were actually going to buy tickets and come and watch us. Perhaps language might be a barrier since we were going to speak in English and Yoruba. Two languages I thought the Spanish speaking clientele may not be too familiar with. I looked up to see about eight people in the audience, and I kept hoping that more would come before the show began. The center was a stickler for time. If only eight people were in the audience, we must perform for them. By the time we began our *Ijuba,* more people joined the eight that I saw, but I was not sure how much they were since they were in the dark and we were all lighted up as performers on stage. We blew the minds of the audience when we were playing *The Tortoise and His Wife*. The Tortoise had gone to the Ifa Priest to ask him for a juju medicine that would make his wife pregnant. The Priest made a delicious porridge laced with juju and asked him to give it to his wife. On the way home, Tortoise ate the porridge that was supposed to be for his wife. So he got pregnant instead of his wife and decided to go back to The Ifa Priest, played by my son, Yinka, to ask for a remedy for his overreaching act. The scene where the Tortoise was crying and begging was hilarious. There was riotous laughter in the audience. They saw what gluttony could do to a person.

My wife and I were only able to realize about one hundred and fifty-six dollars for the La Pena performance. That was after we had taken care of Babatunde, who often acted as if he did not really care about the money. We did not have to worry about ('*Produxion*'), Reuben because he was not our producer for the La Pena performance. The center took their cut out of the ticket sales and their percentage was, of course, bigger than the one that accrued to us.

Right after the La Pena performance, I heard that there was
going to be a big performance in San Francisco, in the Life on the
Water in the Fort Mason Centre. Life on the Water was an upstairs
huge warehouse converted into a theatre, and very well equipped.
The Executive Director, Ellen Sebastian, had gotten grants to fund
the theatre and her theatrical productions. One of the main actors at
The Black Repertory Theatre, Artis Fountain, had told me about the
upcoming stage production. He said that if I was interested, I should
come to the audition, which was going to be at the Fort Mason
Centre in San Francisco, and that the performance was going to be
directed by an African American director, Ellen Sebastian. He said
that she was well known in the Bay Area and that there was some
money involved. I was excited because I thought; finally, I was
going to be in a show that was going to guarantee me some money
regardless of ticket sales. Artis also told me that each actor selected
for the production would receive a contract. My heart missed a beat.
"A contract," I thought, that would be marvelous. However, the
details of the big San Francisco production were still sketchy when
Artis first told me about it. I kept up with him, bugging his phone
every day to the extent of nearly becoming a pest! As soon as he
picked up his phone, he would say something like "Yes Dipo, I
know why you are calling, I haven't heard anything more about the
show, but it sure is going to happen. I'll let you know when I get
more information buddy. Take care man." The next day, of course,
I would call him again, and he would say something like "Didn't
you just call me about this yesterday?" And I would answer that I
was sorry to disturb him again, but a lot could happen in twenty-
four hours especially in show business. I really did not want to tell
him that I thought he might want to keep all the details to himself,
get a juicy part, and a big contract without telling me. I knew,
though, that he would not do a thing like that. He was a very calm
African American man, kind, and compassionate. He was at all the
performances of my plays at the Black Repertory Theatre, offering
constructive criticisms about the plays and the productions. I called

him about a week later, and he was able to give me all the details I wanted.

On the day of the audition, I remember packing my two daughters in my silver colour Volvo car and driving furiously to the Fort Mason Centre in San Francisco where the production was going to take place. It was about February 1988. My wife was about seven months pregnant, and her expected delivery date was in April, she was in no condition to be an actress in a play that would run from April through May 15. The rehearsals would be too gruesome for her, and I did not want her to have the baby on stage! She voluntarily opted out of the audition. My son, who had miraculously jumped on the stage at La Pena to play the role of the Ifa Priest in the *Tortoise and His Wife* folktale, clammed up again and said he did not want to participate in the audition. I told him that they were looking for adult and child actors, but he insisted he was not interested. I even told him that if he was chosen he would be paid, still, the money did not seem of any relevance to him.

When I took my daughters into the huge theatre known as Life on the Water, I was surprised to see Elana Dorsey, there. She played Kike, the girlfriend of the unemployed graduate, Ilori, in my play *The Graduate Palava* that was performed at the Black Repertory Theatre. Artis Fountain was also there. But my biggest surprise was the sight of Luisah Teish, who had been cast in the lead role of Zora Neale Hurston. She hugged me for a long time, and of course lifted my daughter; Buki, off the ground, kissed her and hugged her as well. Buki was the one she was so fond of, and whom she said she wanted to adopt. My wife and I would laugh about it, with my wife saying she was not going to let someone adopt her daughter when she was there to take care of her. I was not sure when Luisah auditioned, but it seemed that on the day I was there for the audition, it had been decided that she would play that lead role. In essence, she just sat with the panel listening to the actors' audition pieces, watching everyone audition. "How is everything Dipo?" She asked itching to know how I was fairing since leaving her Ile Orunmila Oshun. "Fine, fine, we have been doing some performances of Yoruba folk tales in the area," I replied. "Looks like we are going to have a good show," she said to me. "We are going to have a good show?" I was unsure about her statement since my daughters and I had just entered the building and we had not auditioned yet. For all practical purposes, my daughters and I were not members of the cast yet, and we might audition, and not be picked anyway. Perhaps she had mentioned me to the Executive Director, and she had decided she wanted my daughters and me in the production? I rejected that thought as too optimistic and resolved to take a number and wait patiently like the other one hundred actors and actresses waiting to audition for a role in the play. I took my daughters to a section of the auditorium and we sat down. I watched as the red and yellow lights flashed on an actor on stage who was struggling with his lines from Lorraine Hansberry's *A Raisin in the Sun*. I chuckled and said to myself that he had just lost a role in the production, but a voice inside me was saying "what about you? You don't know what you are going to do when you get up there on stage and you just might falter and fail like him". I stopped chuckling and concentrated on my daughters who were pleading with me that I should allow them to go to the bathroom. I tried to tell them that if they called their number and they were not in the auditorium, then they would have missed their slots in the audition line and our scampering out of the house to come to San Francisco for the audition would have been in vain. I watched them squashing their knees together, and with puppy eyes, saying "Please Daddy." The actor sitting next to me looked at them. He seemed to be a white man in his thirties or so. He was dressed in a white shirt, and Khaki pants held up to his shoulders with suspenders. He looked like someone from the 1940s or 1950s era in the United States. He even had a parting separating his hair from the front down to the back of his head. He looked at the girls and looked at me, and then, looked at the girls again. I felt uncomfortable. Here was someone who was going to make me feel bad about insisting that my daughters should just hold on till they had their audition before rushing to the bathroom. Perhaps I was being a bit inconsiderate to two girls who needed to answer the call of nature. But I heard number fourteen, and their numbers were fifteen and sixteen, and mine was seventeen. The 1940s era white man looked at me again, the girls, and then, he looked at me again, tapping his right foot on the ground constantly in such an annoying manner. Then he removed his spectacles to gaze at me as if he was seeing me for the first time. Then, to compound the situation, he got up, straightened his suspenders, adjusted his khaki pants, and started hitting his palm against his thigh, all the time gazing at me amidst the girls' mumblings of "please daddy." Finally, I heard Frances Evens, the Assistant Director say in her almost docile voice which everyone complained about, "number fifteen and sixteen, Bola and Buki". The girls were auditioned together since they were being considered for similar roles in the play. I felt triumphant, at last, I was going to be rid of the 1940s era white man, who was trying to make me feel guilty about insisting that the girls should just wait a minute for their audition before rushing off to the bathroom. As soon as they finished the audition, which was not very long at all maybe about three minutes, they dashed off to go to the bathroom.

I met the director of the impending play, an adaptation of the life and works of the famous African American writer, and anthropologist- Zora Neale Hurston when she met all those she had picked for the play. The 1940s era white man turned out to be Kenn Watt, who was going to play the role of Aaron Schmidt in the play. Like Luisah, it seemed he had been picked before the day my daughters and I auditioned for the play. The director said she was going to stage an adaptation of Hurston's life and work which she called *The Sanctified Church.* She told us to be professional in all our actions, both onstage and offstage. She told us that the production was going to be huge in terms of cast and crew. For example, there were forty-six people in the Production Staff alone, while there were thirty-two people in the cast.

I was cast as Hougan in the upcoming performance. My daughter Buki was cast as Child Dancer, while Bola was cast as a member of the Crow Dancers. I drove home fulfilled. My daughters and I had contracts for a professional production in San Francisco. My contract stipulated that I would be paid eleven hundred dollars, while my two daughters were paid six hundred dollars apiece. Artis Fountain was cast as The Reverend John Hurston, while Elana Dorsey clinched the role of Shouting Woman.

The rehearsals went on very smoothly. I had to drive my daughters to San Francisco for what seemed like endless nights of rehearsals. The nights that I was being rehearsed for my role as the Hougan – a Haitian Voodoo Priest, my daughters, who had no rehearsals on those nights, would go with me anyway. The music for the production was exquisite. It was divided into two; there was the American southern black church music, and the music of Haitian Voodoo, since Zora Neale Hurston dabbled into anthropology, folktale, and spirituality. At one point, I had to train the drummers in the rudiments of African percussion, insisting that they must use the African gong as a time keeper, and a rhythm maker and enhancer for any African derived percussion. Since Haitian Voudou supposedly came from the Republic of Benin, in West Africa, the word itself was from the Fon language spoken there. Because the play was an adaptation of this great American's life and work, the director decided to highlight the spiritual aspect of the writer's work. The audience saw how Zora Neale Hurston was attracted to her father's church in Eatonville, Florida, and how, at the same time, she was attracted to the voodoo religion of Haiti which culminated in her Guggenheim fellowship trip to that country. Some of the songs I enjoyed were from the southern black church of Eatonville, songs like

"Everybody git yo Business Right",
Everybody Git yo Business Right
God told me to tell you git yo business right"

Oh mama come see that crow
See how it flies

That crow, that crow, gonna fly tonight
See how it flies

In the Haitian Section, I enjoyed:

Legua Antibon, Legua Antibon. Legua Antibon
Legua
Nous rive ago ye*
Kore nu entre
Ayida Weddo
Damballah!

*Note: (*This was a song I lead for the Hounsis as the Hougan, that
is, the Chief Voudou*
Priest in the play. Damballah in Haitian Loa is the sky father and
the primordial creator of life. He rules the mind, intellect, and
cosmic equilibrium. He is the Serpent, Spirit and the Great Master
who created the cosmos. He created all the waters of the earth.
There is religious syncretism between Damballah and St. Patrick,
Jesus Christ the Redeemer, Our Lady of Mercy, or Moses.
Damballah's wife is Ayida Weddo, and his concubine is Erzuille
Freda!).

The rehearsals wore on and the play took shape. On the night
of the dress and technical rehearsal, we noticed that Danny Glover,
the African American actor who had been famous for his role as
Albert, in a movie adaptation of Alice Walker's Pulitzer Prize
winning novel, *The Colour Purple*, was there to see the technical
and dress rehearsals. There were plenty of Louisiana food and
drinks in the lobby of the theatre. The table for the main course had
jambalaya, Chitterlings, fried chicken, ham hocks, Crawfish
fettuccine, red beans and rice, corn bread, collard greens, and fried
okra, just to name a few. There were also drinks and dessert tables.
Food and drinks were in abundance and quite tempting. I saw my
daughter Buki, jostling for a spot in front of Danny Glover so she

could scoop up her own mouth-watering jambalaya from the buffet table. Danny let my daughter get in front of him and he just smiled, spoke to her briefly, and waited till she finished, before taking his turn to get his own jambalaya and corn bread. It was an exciting night. He sat in front watching, but soon fell asleep. I was amused. Perhaps he was such a busy movie actor that he only got very little sleep before coming to see our effort that night. I wanted to talk to him or at least land "a connection" with him in Hollywood, but the technical and dress rehearsals wore on virtually all night. I kept looking at him in the front row of the theatre, dosing off intermittently, but I could not leave my place to go and talk to him in a professional production of that nature. When the dress and technical rehearsals were over, I noticed that he had disappeared. I asked my daughter Buki, what Danny had said to her, and she said that he just mentioned to her that there was a lot of food and drinks and that he hoped that she was hungry.

On the day of the performance, I did not really see Danny Glover, perhaps he was there, but I was too charged up and in tune with my character as Hougan – the Haitian Voodoo Priest, to care who was there. It was after the show that I saw that Alice Walker was there. She was riding on the popularity of the movie adaptation of her popular novel – *The Colour Purple*. Luisah Teish was marvellous as Zora Neale Hurston. I had never known her as an actress, but I was impressed. Her role as an inquisitive Zora who became fascinated with Haitian Voudou nearly matched her role in real life as an Oshun Priestess. Even the scene of the possession of the Haitian Hounsis seemed eerily familiar with that of the possession that would have occurred at Ile Orunmila Oshun during an Oshun worship and festival. She played her role with such an easy calm to make me think that she was saying in her mind "I've got this, it is familiar territory, and no one needs to worry about me." She looked majestic on stage, a real Priestess, playing the role of a Priestess!

Artis was outstanding as Reverend John Hurston. He spoke in a very believable southern accent, sometimes, complete with a southern drawl and humour. He handled the language as if it was some exotic food not to be rushed, but to be slowly savoured. The Church Choir was wonderful, with the Church Soloist rendering the song that sent chills up and down the spine of the audience. Some of the actors and production crew decided that they must autograph my own program notes for the production. These were some of what they wrote:

"Dipo, it has been great! We'll be working together again" (Lynne).
Lynne played the role of Magnolia Lee in the production
"Dipo, your spirit, and energy are great. It's been a wonderful evening for me. I thank you for the wonderful moments in your dressing room". (Ken).
Ken played the role of Aaron Schmidt.
"Dipo. We don't seem to understand"*. But it's been loads of fun! Love you" (Jeanne)
Jeanne played the role of Rose Hicks.
(*"We don't seem to understand", **was one of my lines in the play**)
"Dipo, keep your faith in God. It's been great working with you. Keep well." (Al AgiusSinerco).
Al was in charge of recorded sound and music.
"Dipo, I have really enjoyed you and your girls. I hope we work together again soon." (Shakiri)
Shakiri was one of the Haitian Dancers.
"Dipo, I have enjoyed working with you. I hope we do it again." (Aisha)
Aisha was a dancer in the Crow Dance,
"Dipo Faye La Rue. Honour and respect, love. (Elana Dorsey)
Elana played the role of Shouting Woman in the play, and was Kike, in the Black Repertory
Theatre's production of my play- Danger Awake

"Swha, Dipo, you are wonderful. Stay as dynamic as you are and
you will go far" (Hermione) Hermione played the role of one of the
Haitian Hounsis.
"It's deep for the defense. My, my, my, it's been fun. If I on the
trail. I will call deep for the defense. Thanks, Buddy" (Artis
Fountain)
Artis played the heavily demanding role of Reverend John Hurston,
Zora Neale Hurston's father.

After the production of *The Sanctified Church*, I kept hearing rumblings about the show going to a bigger audience in New York, Boston, Chicago, or maybe Los Angeles, the latter city being as close as one could get to Hollywood. Since the Director was going to use the original San Francisco cast, I waited for my phone to ring, and a voice saying to me that the road show was on. Every day, after I got back from my cab driving job, I would check my answering machine to know whether I had gotten a message from Ellen Sebastian, but there would be no message. My son, Abayomi, was born on the tenth of April 1988, two days before the opening of the show! My wife had to stay home for the obligatory period that was necessary to care for the immediate needs of an infant. She was unable to see the show until when it was almost over on the fifteenth of May. My daughters were delighted about their professional act which got them six hundred dollars apiece. With part of the money, they got two wonderful pink jackets which kept them warm during the winter.

I knew that the money I got from the show would not last for ever, so I continued with my cab driving. Although I found it tedious, I knew I could not really tell my wife about that as she was going to conclude that I was just a lazy man who did not want to care for the family. I used to be so shocked at the fares that rode in my cab. I picked up prostitutes, drunks, half-wits, the mentally challenged, bankers, professors, and common street people. At that time, I thought I was going to write a book about my cab driving experience. I actually kept a sort of notebook by my side, and I made entries in it, in between haggling with the obnoxious Dispatcher for a fare or arriving at an address which showed up on the map, but was not in existence in reality! In the 1980s, GPS was not very popular yet, and a cab driver's bible was his "map book". My neighbour, Ajufoh looked at me one day and wondered what I was doing still driving a cab when I had appeared in a pseudo-Hollywood play and all I had to do was just to, according to him, "seize the moment and make it happen". He got on my case more when he heard that I had been in the same room with Alice Walker and Danny Glover. He thought that was my moment, and I had blown it. He was especially disappointed when I told him that I did not get to talk to Danny Glover and consequently, I did not get his number. He looked at me in an unbelievable manner, and I wondered why he was so concerned about me. He grinned mischievously and said, "Why are you still driving a cab?" As for him, I never knew what work he did, other than play around all morning, disappear for a few hours, only to appear in the evening, cooking and playing loud highlife music from Nigeria. His favourite highlife song was *Sweet Mother*, by Prince Nico Mbarga. I knew that he was a great cook, but then, he did not work in any restaurant. He told everyone he was a "Producer" but I had already said that I did not trust him because he was the kind of person who talked so much about doing something but who never did that thing! That was the reason I allowed Ruben Trexidor to be the producer of the Amuyo African folktale theatre performance in San Francisco.

I kept up with the cab driving; I was always given a cab marked "308", a 1984 Chevrolet Monte Carlo. Even if I had called off from driving that day, that cab was always reserved for me somehow, with the dispatcher telling other cab drivers who wanted to grab it that "Hey man that cab is for Dipo." One day, I came in late, and one Mexican-American driver, Jose, had grabbed the key to my cab from the wooden slab on the wall where all other cab keys were hanging. He drove the big Chevrolet out of the parking lot of the company in a hail of smoke, dust, and dripping engine oil. My cab,

308, dripped engine oil badly, but was never fixed and the cab never broke down. I had to jump out of the way to allow Jose maneuver out of the cramped parking lot full of working and non-working cabs. As soon as the Dispatcher saw me he apologized profusely to me that he did not know when Jose grabbed the key to the car and drove off. The Dispatcher coughed, placed his Macdonald's Big Mac dripping with extra Thousand Island dressing on the table, and called Jose on the radio. This was what he said.

Hey, Jose what the fuck? I told you that was Dipo's cab. Why did you pick up the key for 308? That was Dipo's cab man, now he is here in the office, asking for his cab. Hey Jose, you just shut the fuck up and listen to me, bring back 308 right now. What the hell is the matter with you? I ain't got time for your bullshit this afternoon. Bring that cab back right now.

The Dispatcher again apologized to me and even as I was telling him that it was okay that I would drive the Dodge marked 54, I saw Jose driving my Chevrolet back into the Goodwill Cab Company parking lot, munching on a sloppy beef Burrito and Enchilada. I said to myself, "Great, now my cab is going to smell like Burrito and Enchilada." I was not particularly in the mood for that kind of food that day. That was how I got 308 back from Jose. The thing I hated most was the fact that after driving, I had to pay the sixty-eight dollars "gate" as they called it then. One day I made only one hundred dollars all day, and when I paid the sixty-eight dollar gate, I only had about thirty-two dollars left. I did not know how to tell my wife that driving for about thirteen to fourteen hours a day, I only came home with thirty-two dollars!

One day, I was really exasperated about the cab driving as I sat in my cab waiting for a fare at the Oakland International Airport. I pulled out my notebook and wrote the following poem titled: *The Road of 308* .

"308
Come in 308
Highland Psych
What?
I say come in 308
You are breaking
up Where are you
308? You are
breaking up again
San Francisco?
I didn't send you
To San Francisco 308
A huge man
Massive arms
Large torso
Imposing physique
That could make
An elephant jealous
Breaking up
Like 308
Could have crushed a...
If not the wayward god
Who grabbed the thing?
And wrung it
Like wet clothes
Dizzy streets
Or dizzy drivers
Dizzy
driving In
style

Market Street
In the horizon
Yellow metals
Sneaking up
The Embarcadero
Back again on Castro
Where Artists
Disheveled
And wilting
Carve
Objects of beauty
For posterity
A helicopter above
Roaring and
heaving In the
afternoon breeze
Left?
So it is
Radio transmission
Easy Calm
No teacup storm here
Only the tempest
Brewing within
Like morning coffee Grandmother says:
"What one does not see?
Does not irritate"
She should have said
What one does not feel
Does not irritate?

"308 you are breaking up
No breaking up in the back seat
Only easy calm
Boneless man
Scanning the horizon

Designer cap
Covering baldness
Nothing bald in his mind
A luscious forest
Bursting at the edges
With massive trees
308 rise with the sun
Be like the sun
Golden upon a salient turf
Be the easy calm
On East Fourteenth
Be a masquerade
Wrapped around
Dancing his
Dance
In mystic light.

The poem really was a sort of therapy for me. I wrote it after a particular fare I had picked up finally got out of my cab, or better still, jumped out and ran into an alley behind a liquor store, and I had stopped shaking like a common coward. I had picked up an African American drug dealer by accident who ordered me to drive him everywhere in San Francisco. Unknowingly to me, he was hiding a gun in his socks and when he bent down to scratch his leg, I saw the gun. I was afraid when I also saw another gun buried in the gray woolen designer cap he wore. He sat calmly in my cab, and told me to just drive and that he had a lot of money to pay me. He even said that apart from the normal cab fare, he would give me tips to make me, according to him, "dizzy". Apparently, the police had been trailing him, so when he got into my cab, they followed it in their police cruiser, I had picked up a "big drug dealer" and the San Francisco Police Department had ordered a helicopter to follow us as well!

    I heard that the Black Repertory Theatre was going to stage my play *Danger Awake.* It was now about September 1988. I had my hands full helping my wife with our newborn son, and working as a cab driver. I was not sure why the theatre would want to do the play since it had been done at E.G.Y.P.T that year. At any rate, I heard that Deborah Touraine, a very wonderful African American actress I had met at the Black Repertory was really interested in the play. When she phoned me about doing it I told her that as long as she was going to be the Director, I would give my permission. She told me that she really liked the play and that she hoped at least I would come and see it. By that time, of course, my wife and I were planning to move to the Washington D.C. area. I was not really happy about such a move as I saw Washington, D.C., as a city of bureaucrats and politicians, not one of the artists. I did not see the growing and vibrant theatre and movie life of California in a place called Washington D.C. In fact, I had been so used to California that I asked my wife jokingly one day if Washington D.C. was on this planet! My wife wanted us to move to Washington because she thought there would better opportunities for me to get a "real" job, not the theatre and movie jobs I was hustling for in California. To her, I was not being realistic in my artistic endeavours. She mentioned that the family was growing and I had to stop being so "romantic" about the possibilities in the theatre and movie world. Finally, I gave in to her argument and to my disappointment, my wife and I moved out of California in November 1988. However, the Black Repertory Theatre went ahead with their production of my play *Danger Awake.* I kept up with Deborah on the phone and gave her hints concerning the play and how to elicit the dramatic content of the play in production. I taught her some of the Yoruba songs in the play, and particularly, my original compositions such as "*Story Oh! My Story*" and "*The Order to Ponder*". I tried to make her realize the importance of the Ifa priest in the play, and the incantations used by the priest. I told her that the incantations were part therapy, philosophy, and song, often related to the problem for which the priest was seeking a solution.

Deborah sent me a review of the play, which came out of *The Berkeley Voice.* This was part of the review:

"The play begins with a protective prayer by an Ifa priest, whom we meet again, later in the play. He calls forth a play, and the Story Teller, Jennifer Foreman, and her eager listeners begin with song and dance that prepares the audience for the story. The live music, Muata Omolewa on drums and Ava Miller on flute and keyboard are thoroughly delightful, particularly strong dancers Ursala Moon, and Tiffany Pleasant, who twirl around in Nigerian garb with such a gentle intensity that you cannot take your eyes off them. They have a presence. The Story Teller begins the story of Danger, an armed robber sought by the state police, unfortunately, her lengthy introduction with subsequent choral interludes takes a lot of time. Finally, we begin to understand that Danger has been arrested and scheduled for public execution. We finally meet him when he is tied to a tree in a public arena ready for the firing squad. He wears a black mask, a curious theatrical device, often a presentational symbol of evil. The execution scene shifts between political drama and tragedy. The second act is composed mainly of Danger's torment of Lieutenant Goma. The play begins to take off and we actually begin to feel for Goma, we begin to see his struggle and our struggle. There is much talent here and the facility is a dream for a neighbourhood theatre".
(The Berkeley Voice, April 20, 1989.)

As the playwright, I knew it was incumbent upon me to call Deborah and congratulate her on the success of the production, so about a week after I received the review, I called to congratulate her.

Chapter 5: Conclusion.

This account of my years in California only covered the period between 1984 and 1988. I picked this period as a representative snapshot which coincided with my effort at professionalism in my theatrical endeavours. I traced the urge to write this piece to my secondary school (high school) days. It was then that I first discovered my passion for what I often referred to as the three Rs, Reading, Writing, and Running, which I have talked about in an earlier short memoir: *Letters to The Grammarians: Some Memories of Growing Up.* It was in high school, at African Church Grammar School, Ibadan, Nigeria, where I first made up my mind to be a playwright, and a teacher. That feeling has haunted me ever since, and it was not surprising that I finally found myself in that profession.

It is the lessons inherent in this work that drew me to write it. For me, the people, the events, and the situations, all form a huge tapestry of some lessons of life in a very didactic way. Since these lessons were so many and varied, I can only name a few such as: fear, hate, love, trust, friendship, despair, hope, seduction, hunger, homelessness, tenacity, faith, fate, apprehension, professionalism, artistry, loneliness, violence, teaching, learning, disappointment, joblessness, and underemployment. In this conclusion, I will touch on examples of some of these lessons of life as they concern this work.

In the Prologue or The Escape, I presented the root of my escape from a comfortable position as a Lecturer 11 in the Department of Theatre Arts of the University of Calabar. It was this escape, which precipitated my flight back to the United States. It also gave me the urge to take note of those years of my "second coming" (1984-1988). Of course, I had first arrived in the United States in 1971 where I had lived and studied till 1979, that period was my "first coming". It was after this time that I went back to teach in Nigeria for only five short years. One of the lessons here is clear; it was that of fear. I was afraid of the *juju* placed on my chair in my office at the University of Calabar. Fear restricted me to tell only a few trusted people about the incident. My wife was the first to hear about it, then, my wonderful and kind friend, Dr. Ike Nwajei, one of the medical officers of the university clinic. My distant relative Alhaja Konjo and her husband heard about it, and finally, the Ifa Priest who cured me of the evil juju spell. For me, it is human to be "fearful" as the adage says "It is he who runs that lives to fight another day." I do not subscribe to my relative's notion that I should not have been afraid of the juju. For me, that kind of fighting was tantamount to dealing with the metaphysical – a kind of unseen enemies, perhaps, according to the Bible, "principalities", which The Bible describes this way: " *For we wrestle not against flesh and blood, but against "principalities", against powers, against the rulers of the darkness of this world, against spiritual wickedness in high places."* (*The Holy Bible.* Ephesians 6: 12.). My visit to the Ifa priest supports the Yoruba adage "*Epe l'a fi nwepe.*" That is, "It is a curse one employs in curing a curse." The hatred that "the gang of four" had for me precipitated their Machiavellian act and it could have hastened a more portentous consequence. One of them, Nwankwo, in an envious vein, had called me –"the youngest professor from Ilupeju." As lecturers in the department, I was naïve enough to think that we were going to be friends, but I soon found out that was not to be. The essence of love is caring, but the gang of four did not pretend to care, they were a mafia of hate personified. The love Alhaja showed to me helped to save my life in a way despite her sardonic disposition. If I had not trusted her, I would not have gone to her house to seek help for my predicament. She, in turn, showed love and trust by agreeing to be part of the vehicle for my speedy recovery. Even, her incredibly wealthy husband, Alhaji Konjo, who distanced himself at first from my perilous condition, gave "the order" for me to be taken to the Ifa Priest. In this way, he qualified as a friend. He gave hope to a hopeless condition. There was no way I could have known where to go, and I was dodging my extended family; my mother, brothers, and sister. It was the Ifa Priest, who finally gave me hope that I was going to come out of the evil spell. The juxtaposition of the incantations and the sacrifices culminated in the effective cure. Fear prevented me from going back to Calabar to teach in case the gang of four decided to try another form of *juju* on me!

At The Black Repertory Theatre, it was the love Mrs. Vaughn had for me which made her allow me to sleep in the theatre. Really, as a woman of dignity, pride, and consummate goodness, she had made the decision contrary to her husband's edginess on the issue. Staying cold and hungry in the theatre was a real lesson for me. I had been a bit "romantic" about my "second coming" hoping that I would just be welcomed with open hands when I got back to the United States and that I would not have to worry about homelessness, hunger, despair, and even underemployment. Suffering from these negative impulses, I decided not to be broken. I gave artistic support to the Director of *The Father of Secrets*, Steve Jones, and learned a lot from Sam Oni, such as kindness, professionalism, and friendship. He was the one who was so friendly with me, and whom I tried to 'avoid' because of my own inadequacy. As for his vivacious opera singer girlfriend – Mary Dobson, she tried to 'seduce' me, but I managed to avoid that temptation while learning about her appreciation of the opera. The production of my play- *The Father of Secrets* was a different teaching and learning experience for me. I had to teach Steve about the nuances of the Yoruba idioms of the play, and, particularly, the incantations the Ifa Priest, who spoke in incantations almost throughout the play. Watching two rats eat a buffet while I went hungry was an amazing lesson of life for me concerning the importance of the availability of food. It was after that incident that

I decided that people often take the issue of having enough to eat for granted. Imagine finally finding myself in the midst of plenty in Sam Oni's house and gorging myself!

The *Father of Secrets* had been staged in Nigeria, at the Nigerian Television Ibadan, and at the University of Calabar. The revival of sorts, of the play at The Black Repertory Theatre, was a different learning experience for me which added more to my understanding of the human condition. When Marianne, my ex-girlfriend extricated me from the Black Repertory Theatre because she was disgusted that I was sleeping in the theatre, I saw the revival of old friendship. I think I have heard somewhere that "Old friends are better than new." The love she had for me, (no longer the romantic one which ended in 1979), made her insist that I must come and stay in her apartment. My encounter with the father of her young son, "Jahman" the Rastafarian, was a lesson in violence, and how to curb it. I was never a policeman, nor a trained psychologist, but I was able to diffuse Jahman's anger towards Marianne, and the subsequent violent act which ensued. I was elated after Jahman calmed down somewhat and he realized his shortcomings and said: "I've been an asshole man."! I wanted to reply him by saying "Yes, you have been an asshole", but I thought the better of that. Seeing my old professor from Berkeley, Dunbar H. Ogden, at the production of *The Father of Secrets* facilitated another moment for teaching and learning, this time, outside the classroom. During the question and answer session which followed the production, he wanted me to re-write the ending of the play. I had to defend its current ending by diving into some dramatic overtures which precipitated profound laughter from the audience. I proved to him that making the lead character come back to the stage after he was supposed to have left finally would ruin the illusion I was trying to create.

I learned various lessons at Ile Orunmila Oshun. Meeting Luisah Teish again, was itself an experience. She was a woman of remarkable exuberance, charisma, kindness, courage, tenacity, and spirituality. I had known these anyway when we first met in the

1970s. Her house was a juxtaposition of religion, ritual, drama, and feminism. There is a conviction that religion or ritual has a lot to do with drama. I was able to present drama workshops for the Oshun worshippers in her backyard, which I jokingly referred to as "The Courtyard Theatre" since the backyard looked like a courtyard. I was listed in her Calendar as the one who presented the "Drama Workshops." The workshops really were a series of scenes from very religious plays about women. In offering the workshops, the concept of teaching, and learning became important. Particularly, I tried to show the workshop participants, ways to develop their mastery of the nuances of African plays. I also became a "critic of sorts" as I launched a very thorough criticism of Luisah's new book at the time *Jambalaya: The Natural Woman's Book of Personal Charms and Practical Rituals*. I wrote some of the criticisms in my own autographed copy of the book, which I still have today. I learned that to understand the book, one had to immerse one's self into the nature of the feminine condition. That was the learning experience I tried to inculcate into the drama workshops. In fact, I wrote a play called *The Mother of Secrets*, for the drama workshop which we never got to perform before I left Ile Orunmila Oshun. Meeting Baba Fawoye, the Cuban Ifa Priest was another learning experience for me. Just looking at how committed he was to a Yoruba based Santeria/Lucumi religion and his mastery of the Ifa Corpus was a rare feat for me to watch.

The Yoruba language was the basis of Ifa and I was at a loss as to how someone who professed to be a Yoruba Ifa priest could do it without the mastery of the complex Yoruba language. Yet, in Fawoye, I saw hope, commitment, tenacity, faith, trust, and love for the Yoruba religion of Ifa. Despite the incredible handicap of language, I saw an American Ifa priest, who even said he was going to sacrifice a real dog to appease Ogun on behalf of one of his clients- Maggie! Of course, I was a drum teacher and song instructor at Ile Orunmila Oshun as well, teaching Omitolokun the lead drummer, the rudiments of playing the African drum – Djembe. I also taught the female worshippers the Oshun song –

Owu ke Ela ke. In all, love, friendship, tenacity faith, trust, the spiritual prominence of feminism, and the importance of Yoruba Traditional Religion in the United States, were some of the lessons of life I took away from Ile Orunmila Oshun.

At Large in California details my other theatrical endeavours that were to end the period 1984-1988, that is, the end of my sojourn in California. It was in 1988, that I got the role of the Hougan in a professional San Francisco stage production of *The Sanctified Church.* I had moved out of Ile Orunmila Oshun and had gotten an apartment in the building where Ajufoh lived. Apart from my theatre endeavours, I had learned more lessons about love, tolerance, hope, tenacity, artistry, and professionalism. For example, I had to tolerate Ajufoh, or I would have been lured into a fistfight with him and there was no telling how that would have ended. That was an individual who would start punching holes in the walls if the television showed a program he did not like! He got angry on a whim. The love and artistry of Phavia are worth mentioning, and the love and camaraderie of the cast members of *The Sanctified Church* were scintillating. How about Ruben Trexidor- *Produxion?* He was sometimes overzealous, but it was all for a good cause. His tenacity, commitment, and love for a professional stage production were truly heart- warming and invigorating. As a Puerto Rican, he was so much in tune with his African roots, particularly, Yoruba culture, to make a Yoruba from Nigeria jealous!

The cast of my play – *Danger Awake,* provided all the human lessons I enumerated above, and even more. As the Director of the play, I felt like I was the de-facto head of a commune. I had to inculcate love, trust, friendship, teaching, learning, and professionalism, into the group. Jheri, who became someone of ridicule to Ishmail, trusted my judgment and fairness and even listened to my advice. This was what enabled me to suppress the many fights and disagreements, which occurred between him and Ishmail. The Director of a play is a leader. In order to be a leader, one must be willing to face the challenges associated with it. I did not want the commune to crumble, in which case the production will fail, so I had to face the challenges of leadership. Interestingly, experience tells me that even after a stage production ends, the human relationship one has built with the cast and crew endures.

Although there were fights between Ishmail and Jheri, the love, trust, camaraderie, dignity, hope, and professionalism of the group were mesmerizing. They reinforced my hope in the human condition and the fact that these lessons of life are a continuing process of development. Each individual, situation, condition, and time, are steps towards the climb to another level of awareness and realization. Reaching a level is never complete; it is a precursor to the next level. The beauty of the human condition is that it is always in a state of flux; its worst enemy is predictability. It is in this sense that the human condition is a work of art that is open to variant interpretations- something like a huge Italian Renaissance Art sizzling for construal. The individuals, time, situations, and conditions I have described here were basically as I saw or felt them. They remain permanently in the vortex of history. Since history is a conduit to learning, it could be esoteric, especially some of the ones I have described At the Ile Orunmila Oshun. The innate passion for it must be accompanied by a willingness to enter into a certain cryptic essence. I was fully into cab driving when I lived on 35th Avenue in Oakland. The different fares I picked up represent materials for complete books! I was in a unique position to learn some lessons of life from close quarters, for example, I had picked up a female passenger who sat in the back and took off her panties, beckoning to me with her index finger and sticking her tongue out for me to see. I saw all these in the rear view mirror of my Chevrolet Monte Carlo cab- 308. I had to quickly get off the street and park the cab. I know that seduction as I have mentioned earlier is one of the lessons of life, but at that very moment, I knew that seduction would not work without temptation. I refused to be tempted. Other fares rambled on about their profligate lives, and others told me their astounding life stories. I was so enthralled by these "fare stories" I called them at the time that I thought about placing a tape recorder in my cab and just collecting them. Their stories were synonymous with the aspects of the lessons of life I have mentioned. Since "old friends are better than new", I benefited from my friendship with Mrs. Nora B. Vaughn, Luisah Teish, Marianne Lawson, Babatunde Kayode, Johhny Haastrup, Artis Fountain, Elana Dorsey, and others too numerous to name here. My relationship with each individual was like a complete work of art beautiful in essence and divine in composition.

From **The Prologue** to **At Large in California**, I know that I have not included everything that occurred between 1984 and 1988. This is because there is no way I could detail everything; besides, my intention is to feature only "some memories". Perhaps these events will help in the appreciation of the human condition and its capacity to be a repository for teaching and learning.

Printed in the United States
By Bookmasters